Gracious Goodness Around the Table
Breakfast

Darlene Bobo and Kelly Cox

Gracious
Goodness
MINISTRIES

Gracious Goodness Ministries books may be ordered through booksellers or by contacting:

Gracious Goodness Ministries, LLC
P.O. Box 681906
Franklin, TN 37068
www.graciousgoodnessministries.com

ISBN-13: 978-1-968658-01-4

Library of Congress Control Number: 2025913195

Edited by
Rosemary J. Hilliard

Cover and book design by
Mary Elizabeth (M.E.) Hall

Photography by
Darlene Bobo (cover, menu pages, 12, 22, 34, 38, 46, 60, 72, 84, 126, 131, 140, 150, 154)
Kelly Cox (24, 48, 63, 69, 74, 77, 91, 95, 98, 100, 119, 160, 164, 166)
Tim Cox (4, 57, 112, 135, 138)
Kristin Leisman (160)

Dear God the Giver of all blessings and bounty,
We praise you for your grace and goodness.

Bless the hands that prepare this food and let it
nourish the bodies of those who are fed.

Bless the hearts gathered and may each be filled
with the love expressed through this act of
service and your gracious goodness.

Bless the conversations around each table. May
the words spoken bring glory to your Name and
strengthen the mind and soul of each individual.

Thank you for the invitation for us to be gathered
to a place at your table that you have made
possible through the sacrifice of your Son Jesus.

In His name we pray, Amen

Table of Contents

Gracious Goodness Around the Table

Welcome to *Gracious Goodness Around the Table: Breakfast*. This is our first in a series of cookbooks focused on serving others from your kitchen. *Lunch* and *Dinner* will round out the series with each book focusing on specific techniques and methods of taking care of people by serving them delicious food. After all, good food served by those with loving hearts nourishes not only the body, but the heart, mind, and soul as well.

Darlene and Kelly worked together at Butterfly Meadows Inn & Farm in Tennessee for several years. Thousands of guests were served around the table there. You may have been among them. If so, we are pleased to welcome you back to the table within the pages of this book!

Whether you are a new cook or seasoned chef, we have written this book with you in mind. You will find here great and proven recipes that have been adapted from the kitchen at the inn for your home kitchen. Our goal at the inn was to ensure that every meal came out consistently delicious and on time each morning. We know that is your goal as well!

We are sharing with you our comprehensive timeline method for pulling everything together effortlessly. This system was the backbone of our kitchen manual at the inn used to train new cooks and to give seasoned cooks an organizational framework. We know it can work for you too. The timelines have been customized for you to use in your kitchen. Following the timeline will allow you to work at a steady pace instead of a frantic one. Whether you use this book to serve your family, overnight guests, holiday gatherings, or reunions, the timeline method we share here will allow you to enjoy the process and enjoy your guests.

All without setting your hair on fire!

The book is organized into sections by menu. Each menu includes a complete meal with all the recipes to make each dish. The recipes have ingredient charts with serving sizes calculated for you. At a glance you will be able to plan your meal for a few people or a small crowd. You will also find a complete timeline to assist you as you put together each menu.

We always called this system our "paper brain." If you have a good method to follow, you don't have to use brain space to keep the process in your head. You can concentrate on what you are doing and the people around you. And when the people around you ask how they can help, you can assign them a task from where you are currently working in the timeline.

Where to Start? Glad You Asked!

Preparation is the key to any endeavor, and it will save your bacon in the kitchen. Ready to give this a try? Here's our recommended way to approach a menu.

1. First read the timeline. This is your plan of action, so read through the timeline to get an idea in your mind of how the process will flow. Each timeline has been prepared by combining all the steps that need to happen to prepare each menu in the order in which those steps need to happen. Following your menu timeline will remove any guesswork or forgotten steps as you prepare all the dishes. Make note of the steps you can do before the day of serving. We have shared our tricks and tips for preparing items or components of recipes ahead of time. This will make your life in the kitchen so much easier. This is the crucial method for ensuring you don't set your hair on fire!

2. Read each recipe. It's easy for even a seasoned cook to skip over this critical step in preparing a dish. We can all raise a hand to being guilty of this. Take time to read the ingredient list. Look at the notes and hints to see if substitutions for ingredients or equipment are offered. Read the steps to have a feel of the timing and order of each recipe. It will make this familiar territory when you are in the kitchen and things are heating up.

3. Check your pantry and make a shopping list. Make a list of what you need to purchase. Each recipe has an ingredient list. The 1+ day step in the timeline will also have suggestions for items that may not be listed in a recipe. This way you don't forget to have your favorite juice or jam on hand.

4. Assemble the tools and equipment you will need. We have a list at the end of the book of equipment essentials and extras. These are the items that we use to prepare the recipes and any options. You will see that we recommend having a few baking dishes that can be used for preparing even portions for each guest. We found that presenting guests with their own individually prepared dish makes them feel special.

5. *Mise en place* is a French culinary term that literally means to gather or put in place. In the kitchen *mise en place* is used as a noun and verb and a state of mind. If you have completed the above steps, you have set your mind to the task! Now it's time to gather your ingredients for each recipe, measure each ingredient, and THEN begin to follow the recipe instructions. You can set out all the ingredients on your counter for use. Some cooks find it helpful to measure out everything into small prep bowls on a baking sheet. Whatever works for you, taking a moment to put everything in place for each recipe will ensure success in the kitchen.

6. Practice makes perfect or at least very close. We recommend you start with the first menu and prepare it once a week for a month. (You really can serve Sunday Morning French Toast any time or day of the week!) You will find that the process will come naturally by the third or fourth time. Follow the process each month with a new menu and you will have mastered all of the recipes and methods we have shared.

There is an ebb and flow in the kitchen as you are bringing everything together. We call it the kitchen dance. The timelines are the choreography for the dance. So put on some background music and enjoy yourself!

Darlene & Kelly

MENU

Sunday Morning French Toast
Sausage Patties
Mixed Berries
– or –
Sautéed Apples

Sunday Morning French Toast

Ingredients

	Serves 4	Serves 8	Serves 12
Thick Cinnamon Raisin Bread	8 slices	16 slices	24 slices
Eggs	4	8	12
Milk	2½ cups	5 cups	8 cups
Vanilla	½ teaspoon	1 teaspoon	1½ teaspoons
Sugar	2 teaspoons	4 teaspoons	2 Tablespoons
Salt	¼ teaspoon	½ teaspoon	1 teaspoon
Spring and Summer Version			
Butter	4 Tablespoons	8 Tablespoons	12 Tablespoons
Powdered Sugar	2 teaspoons	4 teaspoons	2 Tablespoons

Method

1. Prepare 5 x 7 individual baking dishes or a 9 x 13 baking dish with nonstick cooking spray.

2. Place 2 slices of raisin bread into each individual dish or 8 slices in a 9 x 13 baking dish. If using individual dishes, place them on a baking sheet for easier handling.

3. Using a whisk, mix eggs, milk, vanilla, sugar, and salt in a mixing bowl until well combined. Pour over bread slices.

4. A. Spring and Summer Berry Version: Cut butter into slices, then small pieces. Evenly dot the pieces over the slices of bread.
   B. Fall and Winter Streusel Version: Add streusel topping.

5. Cover dishes with plastic wrap. Place in refrigerator overnight.

6. Remove from the refrigerator half an hour before baking.

7. Bake at 350°F for 40 to 45 minutes. Remove from oven.

8. A. Spring and Summer Berry Version: Using a small strainer, sprinkle powdered sugar over the French toast. Serve with Mixed Berries.
   B. Fall and Winter Streusel Version: Serve with Sautéed Apples.

Hints

One 9 x 13 baking dish is needed per 4 servings.

There will be approximately 1 cup of liquid mixture per serving. If you are using individual dishes, pour 1 cup of the mixture over the bread.

Serve either version with warm maple syrup.

Notes

Mixed Berries

Hints

Adding a little sugar helps bring out the flavor of the berries.

Notes

Ingredients

	Serves 4	Serves 8	Serves 12
Strawberries and/or Raspberries	1½ cups	3 cups	4½ cups
Blueberries and/or Blackberries	1 cup	2 cups	3 cups
Sugar *(optional)*	2 teaspoons	4 teaspoons	6 teaspoons

Method

1. Rinse berries and drain well in a colander.
2. Cut strawberries into pieces similar in size to the other berries and add to a medium mixing bowl.
3. Add the other berries to the mixing bowl.
4. Sprinkle with the sugar and stir gently.
5. Refrigerate until ready to serve.

Streusel Topping

Ingredients

	Serves 4	Serves 8	Serves 12
Brown Sugar *(packed)*	¼ cup	½ cup	¾ cup
Butter	1½ Tablespoons	3 Tablespoons	4½ Tablespoons
Cinnamon	¼ teaspoon	½ teaspoon	¾ teaspoon
Pecans *(chopped)*	¼ cup	½ cup	¾ cup

Method

1. In a medium bowl, mix together brown sugar and cinnamon.

2. Cut butter into small pieces and add to brown sugar mixture.

3. Using a fork or pastry cutter, work the butter into the brown sugar mixture.

4. Mix in the chopped pecans. Crumble the mixture over the French toast before baking. Divide evenly if using individual casserole dishes.

Sautéed Apples

Hints

Stirring apples too frequently or too long will result in applesauce.

Notes

Ingredients

	Serves 4	Serves 8	Serves 12
Granny Smith Apples	2	4	6
Butter	1 Tablespoon	2 Tablespoons	3 Tablespoons
Brown Sugar *(packed)*	4 teaspoons	3 Tablespoons	4½ Tablespoons
Cinnamon	¼ teaspoon	½ teaspoon	¾ teaspoon
Ground Cloves	pinch	pinch	⅛ teaspoon

Method

1. Wash apples, peel and quarter. Remove the core from each quarter, then slice each quarter into 4 slices.

2. In a medium sauté pan, heat butter on medium until bubbly. Add apples and sauté for 5 to 6 minutes.

3. Add brown sugar, cinnamon, and cloves. Cook for 2 more minutes.

4. The apples should be al-dente. Not crunchy, but not mushy either.

Menu Timeline

Prep Actions	Timing

Prep Actions   **Timing**

1. Verify your supply of ingredients. Purchase any items needed to complete each recipe. Note which French toast topping you will prepare. Plan for 2 to 3 pieces of sausage per guest. Remember to add maple syrup to your list.

1+ days

1. Prepare the Sunday Morning French Toast according to the recipe through step 5. Use 5 x 7 baking dishes for individual servings or 9 x 13 baking dish for the number of servings you need. If using individual dishes, prepare 1 casserole per guest following recipe directions. Place the dishes on a large baking sheet for easier handling. Cover dishes with plastic wrap and refrigerate overnight.

2. Remove sausage patties (*2 to 3 per guest*) from freezer. Place in a covered container and refrigerate overnight.

3. Check that your table linens are fresh and clean if you are using these. Set the table adding napkins, flatware, juice glasses, and coffee mugs. Add a selection of sweeteners in a dish, as well as salt and pepper shakers.

4. Run the dishwasher so you begin tomorrow with clean dishes and an empty dishwasher ready for the breakfast dishes.

24+ hours

1. Turn on coffee maker. Turn on lights and music for a nice atmosphere for the cook and the guests.

2. Take French toast out of the refrigerator and place on the counter so the dishes can come to room temperature. Allowing the dishes to come to room temperature will help prevent them from breaking when placed in a hot oven.

3. Thaw sausage if this was not done the day before.

2 hours

Menu Timeline

Timing	Prep Actions

Timing

Prep Actions

1 **45**
hour min

1. Pour juices and water into pitchers. Keep in the refrigerator until serving.
2. Set the table if this was not done the day before.
3. Empty clean dishes from the dishwasher.
4. Make a pot of coffee for the cook and early risers.

1 **30**
hour min

1. Preheat oven to 350°F.
2. A. For the Spring and Summer Berry version, prepare berries according to the recipe. Spoon the berries into a small ramekin or bowl for each guest. Place in refrigerator until ready to serve.

   B. For the Fall and Winter Streusel version, prepare apples according to the recipe. Take care not to overcook the apples. Spoon the apples into a small ramekin or bowl for each guest. Do not refrigerate the apples.

1
hour

1. Remove plastic wrap from baking dishes.
2. Place French toast in the oven.
3. Pour maple syrup into a small pitcher and place in a bowl or pan of warm water.
4. Take a moment to put away the ingredients you have finished using. Put used dishes and utensils into the dishwasher.

Menu Timeline

Prep Actions	Timing

1. Cook sausage patties *(2 or 3 per guest)* according to package directions. Place patties in a small ovenproof dish. Cover with foil to keep warm.

2. Check French toast. Rotate baking sheets or 9 x 13 baking dish from top to bottom racks and back to front for even baking.

3. Set out the plates. Add a small napkin or washable coaster to the plate if using individual casserole dishes. This keeps the dish from slipping on the plate.

30 min

1. Place juices, water, warm maple syrup, and creamer on the table.

2. Place a berry dish or apple dish at each place setting.

20 min

1. Remove French toast from oven and place the individual casserole dish on the plate. If using a 9 x 13 baking dish, slice French toast into 4 portions and place 1 portion on each plate.

2. If serving the berry option, sprinkle French toast with powdered sugar using a small strainer.

3. Place sausages on each plate or a platter for passing at the table.

10 min

1. Serve each guest a beautiful plate.

2. Offer coffee or tea.

0 ready

MENU

Crustless Spinach Quiche
with Fresh Tomatoes

Biscuits with Country Ham

Roasted Sweet Potatoes

Mini Strawberry
Chocolate Chip Muffins

Crustless Spinach Quiche

Ingredients

	Serves 8	Serves 16	Serves 24
Butter	2 Tablespoons	3 Tablespoons	4 Tablespoons
Fresh Cremini Mushrooms	1 pound	2 pounds	3 pounds
Scallions (*chopped*)	½ cup	1 cup	1½ cups
Spinach (*chopped*)	3 cups	6 cups	9 cups
Eggs	12	24	36
Cottage Cheese	2 cups	4 cups	6 cups
Sharp Cheddar Cheese (*shredded*)	2 cups	4 cups	6 cups
Salt	¼ teaspoon	½ teaspoon	¾ teaspoon
Pepper	¼ teaspoon	½ teaspoon	¾ teaspoon
Croutons (*rough chopped*)	1 cup	2 cups	3 cups

Method

1. Preheat oven to 350°F.

2. Clean mushrooms with a damp paper towel or a soft brush and then slice. Chop scallions and spinach. Set aside in separate bowls.

3. In a large skillet, heat butter on high until bubbly.

4. Add sliced mushrooms and sauté until cooked, approximately 2 to 3 minutes.

5. Remove from heat. Add scallions and spinach. Mix well.

6. In a separate bowl, mix eggs, cottage cheese, sharp cheddar cheese, salt, and pepper until well combined.

7. Add vegetables to the egg mixture. Stir until well mixed.

8. Pour 1 cup portions into greased 10 ounce oven safe dishes. Place dishes on a baking sheet for easier handling. (*Mixture can be frozen at this step. See Hints.*)

Hints

This dish is great to have stored in the freezer ready for a quick and easy meal. Prepare and freeze in 2 cup portions (1 cup equals 1 serving). Thaw the number of servings you need the night before and bake for breakfast the next morning.

Paired with a salad, this quiche is also an option for an easy and delicious dinner.

Notes

9. Bake at 350°F for 45 minutes. Quiche will be lightly brown and puffed up when done.

10. Sprinkle an equal portion of chopped croutons on top of each quiche after removing from the oven. Serve hot.

Biscuits

Ingredients

	Makes 12	Makes 25	Makes 50
All Purpose Flour	1 cup	2 cups	4 cups
Baking Powder	1 teaspoon	2 teaspoons	4 teaspoons
Baking Soda	¼ teaspoon	½ teaspoon	1 teaspoon
Salt	¼ teaspoon	½ teaspoon	1 teaspoon
Salted Butter	3 Tablespoons	6 Tablespoons	12 Tablespoons
Sour Cream	½ cup	1 cup	2 cups
Milk	1½ Tablespoons	3 Tablespoons	⅓ cup
Basting			
Salted Butter *(melted)*	4 Tablespoons	8 Tablespoons	12 Tablespoons

Method

1. Preheat oven to 400°F. Line a baking sheet with parchment paper.

2. Using a whisk, mix the flour, baking powder, baking soda, and salt in a medium bowl until well combined.

3. Slice the butter into tablespoon-size pieces and add to the flour mixture.

4. Using a pastry cutter, cut butter pieces into the dry ingredients until the butter is pea-size.

5. Add sour cream and milk. Mix until incorporated. Let rest for 10 minutes.

6. Roll out dough to 1 inch thickness on a lightly floured surface.

7. Using a round cutter or small juice glass, cut dough into 2 inch circles. Place on prepared baking sheet.

8. Bake at 400°F on middle rack for 5 minutes. Remove from oven and baste *(brush)* tops with melted butter. Rotate the baking sheet back to front and place on top rack in oven to ensure a nicely browned biscuit top.

9. Bake for 5 to 7 more minutes. The edges will be golden brown when done and the middle will spring back when touched lightly.

Hints

You can freeze the raw biscuits after they are cut by placing them in a single layer on a baking sheet lined with parchment paper. Place in the freezer 2 hours. Do not stack baking sheets. Store the frozen biscuits in an airtight container or large zip freezer bag.

Serve biscuits with apple butter or jam and softened butter.

Notes

Roasted Sweet Potatoes

Hints

Raw sweet potatoes are very hard. Take care when peeling and dicing.

Notes

Ingredients

	Serves 6	Serves 12	Serves 24
Sweet Potatoes	3 large	6 large	12 large
Olive oil	2 Tablespoons	¼ cup	½ cup
Salt	¾ teaspoon	1½ teaspoons	3 teaspoons
Pepper	½ teaspoon	1 teaspoon	2 teaspoons

Method

1. Preheat oven to 350°F. Line a baking sheet with parchment paper.

2. Wash potatoes and pat dry.

3. Peel and small dice sweet potatoes. *(Approximately ½ sweet potato per guest. This will result in ¾ to 1 cup of potato cubes per guest.)*

4. In a large bowl, toss the diced potatoes with the olive oil, salt, and pepper.

5. Evenly scatter the sweet potatoes over prepared baking sheet.

6. Bake at 350°F for 45 to 50 minutes. Stir potatoes and rotate baking sheet every 15 minutes.

Mini Strawberry Chocolate Chip Muffins

Ingredients

	Makes 20	Makes 30	Makes 40
All Purpose Flour	2 cups	3 cups	4 cups
Sugar	1 cup	1½ cups	2 cups
Baking Soda	½ teaspoon	¾ teaspoon	1 teaspoon
Baking Powder	1½ teaspoons	2¼ teaspoons	3 teaspoons
Milk	¾ cup	1¼ cups	1½ cups
Vegetable Oil	4 Tablespoons	6 Tablespoons	8 Tablespoons
Eggs	1	2	2
Strawberries (small diced)	1 cup	1½ cups	2 cups
Chocolate Chips (mini)	½ cup	¾ cup	1 cup

Hints

The dry and wet ingredients should be mixed together only until just combined. Overmixing the batter will result in baked muffins with a tough texture.

A squeeze release scoop is handy for filling muffin pans. A 2 Tablespoon (#40) scoop fills a mini size muffin pan perfectly. There is less mess too!

Any empty muffin wells may be half-filled with water to keep the pan from warping in a hot oven.

Notes

Method

1. Preheat oven to 350°F. Prepare muffin pans with nonstick baking spray or paper liners.

2. Using a whisk, mix flour, sugar, baking soda, and baking powder in a large mixing bowl until well combined.

3. In a separate bowl, mix milk, oil, and egg(s). Add to the flour mixture and mix until just combined.

4. Gently fold in the chopped strawberries and mini chocolate chips.

5. Scoop batter into prepared mini muffin pans.

6. Bake at 350°F for 20 minutes or until lightly golden brown. The center of the muffin will spring back with a gentle press to the top when done.

7. Allow to cool. Remove from pans and serve (2 per guest).

8. These muffins are best made the day of or the day before serving.

Menu Timeline

Timing	Prep Actions

Timing

1+
days

24+
hours

Prep Actions

1. Verify your supply of ingredients. Purchase any items needed to complete each recipe. Include some apple butter or jam for the biscuits.
2. It is helpful to have the biscuits prepared ahead. Prepare and freeze unbaked biscuits according to the recipe up to 1 month before baking.
3. Spinach Quiche mixture can be prepared ahead and frozen for 1 month. Do not bake mixture prior to freezing. Freezing in 2 cup portions will allow for two 1 cup servings in individual ramekins.

1. Prepare Mini Strawberry Chocolate Chip Muffins according to the recipe. Cool completely and store in an airtight container on the counter.
2. Thaw or prepare the quiche mixture. Add mixture to prepared individual oven safe bowls or ramekins. Place the bowls or ramekins on a large baking sheet for easier handling. Cover with plastic wrap and refrigerate overnight.
3. Check that your table linens are fresh and clean if you are using these. Set the table adding napkins, flatware, juice glasses, and coffee mugs. Add a selection of sweeteners in a dish, as well as salt and pepper shakers.
4. Run the dishwasher so you begin tomorrow with clean dishes and an empty dishwasher ready for all of the breakfast dishes.

Menu Timeline

Prep Actions

1. Turn on coffee maker. Turn on lights and music for a nice atmosphere for the cook and the guests.
2. Remove biscuits from the freezer *(1 per guest)*. Place on a baking sheet lined with parchment paper.
3. Place muffins *(2 per guest)* on a separate baking sheet lined with parchment paper and cover with foil.

Timing: 2 hours

1. Pour juices and water into pitchers. Keep in the refrigerator until serving.
2. Set the table if this was not done the day before.
3. Empty clean dishes from the dishwasher.
4. Make a pot of coffee for the cook and early risers.

Timing: 1 hour 45 min

1. Preheat oven to 350°F.
2. Take quiche out of the refrigerator and place on the counter so the dishes can come to room temperature. Allowing the dishes to come to room temperature will help prevent them from breaking when placed in a hot oven.
3. Prepare sweet potatoes according to recipe.

Timing: 1 hour 30 min

Menu Timeline

Timing	Prep Actions
1 hour	1. Place quiche and sweet potatoes in the 350°F oven. 2. Slice tomatoes, place on papertowel, and sprinkle with salt. Refrigerate until plating.
45 min	1. In a skillet with a little bit of water added, begin heating biscuit-size pieces of country ham. Cook ham according to package directions. Place slices in a small ovenproof dish. Cover with foil to keep warm. 2. Set out the plates. Add a small napkin or washable coaster to the plate for the individual casserole dishes. This keeps the dish from slipping on the plate. 3. Take a moment to put away the ingredients you have finished using. Put used dishes and utensils into the dishwasher.
30 min	1. Rotate the baking sheet with the quiche back to front for even baking. 2. Stir the sweet potatoes. 3. Melt butter for the biscuits.
20 min	1. Raise oven temperature to 400°F. 2. Stir the sweet potatoes.

Menu Timeline

Prep Actions	Timing

Prep Actions · **Timing**

1. Remove quiche and potatoes from oven.
2. Place biscuits in the oven for 5 minutes.
3. Place muffins in the oven for 3 to 4 minutes to warm. To avoid overheating, set a timer for 4 minutes.
4. Remove muffins from oven.

15 min

1. Remove biscuits from oven and brush tops with melted butter. Rotate the baking sheet back to front and move to the top rack for 5 to 7 minutes until biscuits are golden brown.
2. Place juices, water, and creamer on the table.

10 min

1. Remove biscuits from oven.
2. Slice a biscuit and add a piece of county ham *(1 per guest)*.
3. Prepare each plate with a serving of quiche, ½ to ¾ cup of potatoes, and a country ham biscuit.
4. Add 2 muffins to each plate. Or place muffins in a towel-lined breadbasket or bowl to serve from the table.
5. Add tomato slices to each plate.

5 min

1. Serve each guest a beautiful plate.
2. Offer coffee or tea.

0 ready

MENU

Three Cheese Western Omelet
Baked Cheese Grits
Chicken Sausage
Tomatoes
Cinnamon Muffins
Tea Biscuits

Three Cheese Western Omelet

Ingredients

	Serves 6	Serves 12	Serves 24
Salsa	½ cup	1 cup	2 cups
Artichoke Hearts (quartered)	1 cup	2 cups	4 cups
Sharp Cheddar Cheese (shredded)	1 cup	2 cups	4 cups
Parmesan Cheese (shredded)	½ cup	1 cup	2 cups
Monterey Jack Cheese (shredded)	¾ cup	1½ cups	3 cups
Chives (chopped)	1 Tablespoon	2 Tablespoons	¼ cup
Eggs	8	16	32
Sour Cream	1 cup	2 cups	4 cups
Salt	¼ teaspoon	½ teaspoon	1 teaspoon
Pepper	¼ teaspoon	½ teaspoon	1 teaspoon
Cumin (optional)	⅛ teaspoon	¼ teaspoon	½ teaspoon

Hints

This is nice cut into wedges to serve.

Notes

Method

1. Preheat oven to 350°F. Prepare a 10 inch pie plate with nonstick cooking spray.
2. Drain excess liquid from salsa, then spread salsa evenly over the bottom of prepared pie plate.
3. Drain artichoke hearts and pat dry with a paper towel. Spread artichoke hearts over the salsa.
4. Sprinkle cheeses over artichoke hearts and salsa.
5. In a medium mixing bowl, mix eggs, sour cream, chives, salt, pepper, and cumin (optional) until well combined.
6. Pour egg mixture over cheeses.
7. Bake at 350°F for 35 to 40 minutes. The top will be slightly brown and the sides will be bubbling when done.

Baked Cheese Grits

Hints

This can also be prepared in a baking dish and cut into portions for serving.

An 8 x 8 baking dish can be used for 6 servings. A 9 x 13 baking dish will be needed for 12 servings.

Grits can pop and splatter while cooking. Use a pot large enough to have 2 to 3 inches of space above the cooking grits. This helps keep them in the pot and off your stovetop!

Notes

Ingredients

	Serves 6	Serves 12	Serves 24
Water	3 cups	6 cups	12 cups
Quick Grits	¾ cup	1½ cups	3 cups
Salt	¼ teaspoon	½ teaspoon	1 teaspoon
White Pepper	dash	⅛ teaspoon	¼ teaspoon
Eggs	1	2	4
Sharp Cheddar Cheese (*shredded*)	1 cup	2 cups	4 cups
Butter	2 Tablespoons	4 Tablespoons	8 Tablespoons
Garnish			
Sharp Cheddar Cheese (*shredded*)	¼ cup	½ cup	1 cup

Method

1. Preheat oven to 350°F. Prepare individual ramekins or baking dish with nonstick cooking spray.

2. Place water and salt into a large pot and bring to a boil.

3. Whisk in the grits slowly making sure to incorporate them fully into the liquid. Reduce heat and cook until thick. Whisk often to ensure there are no lumps.

4. In a medium bowl, beat egg(s) with a fork. Add a small amount of grits to the egg(s) and stir vigorously. This step keeps the egg(s) from immediately cooking and lumping up in the hot grits.

5. Add the egg mixture to the original pot of grits and stir.

6. Add the white pepper, butter, and cheese. Stir to mix well.

7. Cook over low heat, stirring until cheese is melted and all ingredients are well combined. Remove from heat.

8. Pour or scoop into prepared ramekins or baking dish.

9. Bake at 350°F for 30 minutes until top is set and lightly puffed. Garnish with a sprinkle of cheese. Let stand for 5 minutes before serving.

Cinnamon Muffins

Ingredients

	Makes 12	Makes 24	Makes 36
All Purpose Flour	2 cups	4 cups	6 cups
Sugar	¾ cup	1½ cups	2¼ cups
Baking Powder	2¼ teaspoons	4½ teaspoons	7 teaspoons
Salt	¾ teaspoon	1½ teaspoons	2¼ teaspoons
Nutmeg	¼ teaspoon	½ teaspoon	1 teaspoon
Cinnamon	¼ teaspoon	½ teaspoon	1 teaspoon
Butter	4 ounces (1 stick)	8 ounces (2 sticks)	12 ounces (3 sticks)
Eggs	2	3	5
Milk	¾ cup	1½ cups	2¼ cups
Topping			
Butter	2 Tablespoons	4 Tablespoons	6 Tablespoons
Sugar	¼ cup	½ cup	¾ cup
Cinnamon	½ teaspoon	1 teaspoon	1½ teaspoons

Hints

The dry and wet ingredients should be mixed together only until just combined. Overmixing the batter will result in baked muffins with a tough texture.

A squeeze release scoop is handy for filling muffin pans. A ½ cup (#8) scoop fills a regular size muffin pan perfectly. There will be less mess too!

Any empty muffin wells may be half-filled with water to keep the pan from warping in a hot oven.

Notes

Method

1. Preheat oven to 350°F. Prepare muffin pans with nonstick baking spray or paper liners.

2. Melt the first measurement of butter and set aside.

3. Using a whisk, mix flour, sugar, baking powder, salt, nutmeg, and cinnamon in a large mixing bowl until well combined. Set aside.

4. In a medium mixing bowl, mix eggs, milk, and the first measurement of melted butter. Add to the dry ingredients. Mix until just combined.

5. Scoop batter into prepared muffin pans.

6. Bake at 350°F for 15 minutes or until lightly golden brown. The center of the muffin will spring back with a gentle press to the top when done.

Notes

7. The muffins can be prepared the day before serving. You may also prepare up to 1 month ahead and store in an airtight container in the freezer. Let the muffins cool completely before storing.

8. Topping: Just prior to serving, while the muffins are baking or heating, melt the second measurement of butter in a small pan or bowl.

9. In a separate small bowl, combine the sugar and cinnamon for the topping. Set aside.

10. Once muffins come out of the oven, brush with melted butter and dip into the cinnamon sugar mixture. (*This step should be done just prior to serving if muffins were thawed from frozen or baked the day before.*)

Tea Biscuits

Quick Biscuit Mix

	Makes 3 Cups	Makes 6 Cups	Makes 12 Cups
All Purpose Flour	2½ cups	5 cups	10 cups
Baking Powder	4½ teaspoons	3 Tablespoons	6 Tablespoons
Cornstarch	¼ cup	½ cup	1 cup
Sugar	1 Tablespoon	2 Tablespoons	¼ cup
Salt	½ teaspoon	1 teaspoon	2 teaspoons
Cold Butter	4 ounces (1 stick)	8 ounces (2 sticks)	16 ounces (4 sticks)

Method

1. Using a whisk, mix flour, baking powder, cornstarch, sugar, and salt in a large bowl until well combined.

2. Slice butter into tablespoon-size pieces and add to the flour mixture. Using a pastry cutter, cut butter pieces into the dry ingredients until the butter is tiny pea-size. Place in an airtight container and freeze for 2 months.

Tea Biscuits

	Makes 12	Makes 24	Makes 48
Butter	2 ounces (½ stick)	4 ounces (1 stick)	8 ounces (2 sticks)
Sour Cream	½ cup	1 cup	2 cups
Quick Biscuit Mix	1 cup	2 cups	4 cups

Method

1. Preheat oven to 375°F. Prepare mini muffin pan with nonstick baking spray. Melt butter.

2. In a medium mixing bowl, add biscuit mix, sour cream, and melted butter. Stir to incorporate all ingredients.

3. Scoop batter into prepared mini muffin pan.

4. Bake at 375°F for 8 to 10 minutes or until lightly golden brown.

Hints

Jam is nice to serve with these biscuits.

A squeeze release scoop is handy for filling muffin pans. A 2 Tablespoon (#40) scoop fills a mini size muffin pan perfectly. There is less mess too!

Purchased dry biscuit/pancake mix can be substituted for the Quick Biscuit Mix.

Notes

Menu Timeline

Timing	Prep Actions

Timing

Prep Actions

1+
days

1. Verify your supply of ingredients. Purchase any items needed to complete each recipe. Chicken sausage links may be refrigerated or frozen until ready to prepare. Have some jam on hand to serve with the tea biscuits.
2. Tea Biscuits and Cinnamon Muffins can be prepared, baked, and frozen up to 1 month ahead.
3. Cinnamon sugar for the muffin topping may be prepared ahead and kept in an airtight container.

24+
hours

1. Remove chicken sausage *(1 per guest)* from the freezer. Place in an airtight container in the refrigerator to thaw overnight.
2. Prepare muffins and tea biscuits according to each recipe. If these were previously prepared and frozen, remove muffins *(1 per guest)* and tea biscuits *(2 per guest)* from the freezer. Place in an airtight container on the counter.
3. Shred cheeses according to each recipe for the number of servings needed. For example, shred ¾ cup Monterey Jack, 2 cups sharp cheddar, and ½ cup Parmesan cheese for 6 servings of Three Cheese Western Omelet and Baked Cheese Grits.
4. Cheese grits can be prepared according to recipe through step 9. Do not bake. Place in prepared individual ramekins or baking dish and allow to cool. Cover with plastic wrap and refrigerate overnight.
5. Check that your table linens are fresh and clean if you are using these. Set the table adding napkins, flatware, juice glasses, and coffee mugs. Add a selection of sweeteners in a dish, as well as salt and pepper shakers.
6. Run the dishwasher so you begin tomorrow with clean dishes and an empty dishwasher ready for all of the breakfast dishes.

Menu Timeline

Prep Actions		Timing

Prep Actions

1. Turn on coffee maker. Turn on lights and music for a nice atmosphere for the cook and the guests.
2. Shred cheeses if you did not do this the day before. Remember to shred enough for the grits and omelet.
3. Thaw sausages, muffins, and tea biscuits if this was not done the day before. Place muffins and tea biscuits on a baking sheet lined with parchment paper and cover with foil.

2 hours

1. Pour juices and water into pitchers. Keep in the refrigerator until serving.
2. Set the table if this was not done the day before.
3. Empty clean dishes from the dishwasher.
4. Make a pot of coffee for the cook and early risers.

1 hour **45** min

1. Prepare the western omelet according to recipe. It is important to drain the salsa and pat dry the artichokes with paper towels.
2. Slice tomatoes, place on paper towel, and sprinkle with salt. Refrigerate until plating.

1 hour **30** min

1. Preheat oven to 350°F.
2. Prepare the grits if this was not done the day before.
3. If the grits were prepared the day before, remove ramekins or baking dish from the refrigerator and place on the counter so the dishes can come to room temperature. Allowing the dishes to come to room temperature will help prevent them from breaking when placed in a hot oven.

1 hour **15** min

Menu Timeline

Timing	Prep Actions
1 hour	1. Place omelet in the oven. 2. Take a moment to put away the ingredients you have finished using. Put used dishes and utensils in the dishwasher.
45 min	1. Place grits in the oven. 2. In a large skillet, cook chicken sausages according to package directions. Place sausages into small ovenproof dish. Cover with foil to keep warm.
30 min	1. Rotate grits and omelet top to bottom and back to front in the oven for even baking. 2. Set out the plates.
20 min	1. Place muffins and tea biscuits in oven for 5 to 7 minutes to warm. To avoid overheating, set a timer for 7 minutes. 2. Melt butter in a small pan. Place cinnamon sugar mixture in a bowl. 3. Remove muffins and tea biscuits from oven. 4. Brush warm muffin tops with the melted butter and dip into the cinnamon sugar.

Menu Timeline

Prep Actions	Timing
1. Place juices, water, and creamer on the table. 2. Remove grits and omelet from the oven. Let omelet rest 5 minutes, then cut into serving portions.	**15** min
1. Prepare each plate with a serving of omelet, grits, and a sausage. 2. Add a muffin and 2 tea biscuits to each plate. Or place these in a towel-lined breadbasket or bowl and place on the table. 3. Add tomato slices to each plate.	**5** min
1. Serve each guest a beautiful plate. 2. Offer coffee or tea.	**0** ready

MENU

Oatmeal Brûlée
Scrambled Eggs
Banana Walnut Muffins
Cinnamon Raisin Toast
Bacon
Mixed Fruit

Oatmeal Brûlée

Ingredients

	Serves 4	Serves 8	Serves 16
Water	3 cups	6 cups	12 cups
Steel Cut Irish Oats	1 cup	2 cups	4 cups
Cinnamon	1 teaspoon	2 teaspoons	4 teaspoons
Salt	pinch	¼ teaspoon	½ teaspoon
Raw Sugar (*topping*)	½ cup	1 cup	2 cups
Brown Sugar (*placed in a bowl*)	½ cup	1 cup	2 cups
Craisins (*placed in a bowl*)	½ cup	1 cup	2 cups
Toasted Walnuts (*placed in a bowl*)	½ cup	1 cup	2 cups

Hints

Steel Cut Irish Oats are whole oats chopped more coarsely than rolled oats. Steel cut oats have a nuttier taste and chewier texture than other types of oats.

Raw Sugar or turbinado cane sugar is a less processed form of sugar retaining a darker molasses color and flavor.

Notes

Method

1. Preheat oven to 350°F. Line a baking sheet with parchment paper.

2. Place walnuts on prepared baking sheet. Bake at 350°F for 6 to 8 minutes, then set aside. Set a timer as these can quickly burn.

3. Boil water in a medium sauce pan.

4. When the water comes to a brisk boil, add the oats. Stir as you add the oats to the water to keep them from sticking together and becoming lumpy. Reduce the heat to low. Simmer uncovered for 25 minutes stirring frequently.

5. Prepare 10 ounce oven safe bowls with a nonstick cooking spray. Place dishes on a baking sheet for easier handling.

6. Preheat oven to Broil (500°F).

7. Add the cinnamon and salt to the oats and mix well.

8. Add approximately 1 cup of oatmeal to each prepared bowl.

9. Generously sprinkle the raw sugar over the top of the oatmeal.

10. Place the dishes of oatmeal under the broiler until sugar is bubbly. Watch carefully, this will only take 2 to 5 minutes.

11. Cool slightly. Serve with the bowls of brown sugar, craisins, and toasted walnuts for toppings.

Scrambled Eggs

Ingredients

	Serves 4	Serves 8	Serves 16
Eggs	4	8	16
Milk	4 teaspoons	3 Tablepoons	⅓ cup
Salt	¼ teaspoon	½ teaspoon	1 teaspoon
Pepper	¼ teaspoon	½ teaspoon	1 teaspoon
Butter	1 Tablespoon	2 Tablespoons	4 Tablespoons

Method

1. Break eggs into a bowl and whisk vigorously until well incorporated.

2. Add milk, salt, and pepper. Mix well.

3. In a large skillet, heat butter on medium low until bubbly.

4. Once butter is hot and bubbly, add egg mixture to the pan.

5. Cook eggs without stirring until mixture begins to set on bottom. Using a large spatula, carefully scrap sides and bottom of the pan to allow uncooked eggs to flow to bottom. Repeat as eggs cook to form scrambled texture. Avoid stirring constantly.

6. Once eggs are cooked but still look slightly wet, remove from heat and let rest for 2 to 3 minutes.

7. Serve hot.

Banana Walnut Muffins

Hints

The dry and wet ingredients should be mixed together only until just combined. Overmixing the batter will result in baked muffins with a tough texture.

A squeeze release scoop is handy for filling muffin pans. A ½ cup (#8) scoop fills a regular size muffin pan perfectly. There will be less mess too!

Any empty muffin wells may be half-filled with water to keep the pan from warping in a hot oven.

Be sure to use ripe bananas to mash and add to the mixture.

The muffins can be prepared the day before serving. You may also prepare up to 1 month ahead and store in an airtight container in the freezer. Let the muffins cool completely before storing.

Ingredients

	Makes 20	Makes 30	Makes 40
Butter (room temperature)	4 Tablespoons	6 Tablespoons	8 Tablespoons
Sugar	1⅓ cups	2 cups	2⅔ cups
Eggs	2	3	4
Mashed Banana	1 cup	1½ cups	2 cups
Sour Cream	1 cup	1½ cups	2 cups
Vanilla Extract	1 teaspoon	1½ teaspoons	2 teaspoons
All Purpose Flour	2 cups	3 cups	4 cups
Baking Soda	1 teaspoon	1½ teaspoons	2 teaspoons
Baking Powder	1 teaspoon	1½ teaspoons	2 teaspoons
Salt	¼ teaspoon	¼ teaspoon	½ teaspoon
Chopped Walnuts	½ cup	¾ cup	1 cup

Method

1. Preheat oven to 325°F. Prepare muffin pans with nonstick baking spray or paper liners. Line a baking sheet with parchment paper.

2. Place walnuts on the baking sheet. Bake at 325°F for 5 to 7 minutes. Set a timer as these can quickly burn. Set aside to cool.

3. In a large mixing bowl, cream butter and sugar with hand mixer. Add eggs one at a time and mix until well incorporated.

4. Add mashed banana, sour cream, and vanilla extract. Continue to beat together until thoroughly mixed and slightly fluffy. Set aside.

5. Using a whisk, mix flour, baking soda, baking powder, and salt in a medium mixing bowl until well combined.

6. Add flour mixture to the banana mixture. Mix by hand until just combined.

7. Fold in walnuts. Scoop batter into muffin pans.

8. Bake at 325°F for 20 minutes or until a toothpick inserted at the center comes out clean.

Cinnamon Raisin Toast

Ingredients

	Makes 4	Makes 8	Makes 16
Raisin Bread	4 slices	8 slices	16 slices
Cinnamon Butter			
Butter (softened)	2 ounces (½ stick)	4 ounces (1 stick)	8 ounces (2 sticks)
Sugar	¼ cup	½ cup	1 cup
Cinnamon	1 teaspoon	2 teaspoons	4 teaspoons
Vanilla Extract	1 teaspoon	2 teaspoons	4 teaspoons
Nutmeg	pinch	dash	⅛ teaspoon

Hints

Cinnamon butter can be prepared and stored in an airtight container in the refrigerator for 1 month. Soften before using.

Notes

Method

1. Preheat oven to 350°F. Line a baking sheet with parchment paper.

2. Using a hand mixer, combine the butter, sugar, cinnamon, vanilla, and nutmeg in a medium mixing bowl. Scrape down the sides of the bowl several times with a spatula while mixing to incorporate all the butter.

3. Spread the cinnamon butter on the slices of bread. Make sure to cover the entire slice to the edges.

4. Place each slice butter side up on prepared baking sheet.

5. Bake at 350°F for 5 to 10 minutes depending on the thickness of bread slices.

6. Switch oven to the broiler setting. Warning! Only leave the toast under the broiler for 1 to 2 minutes and watch constantly to make sure the toast does not burn.

7. Remove toast from the oven, cut diagonally in half and serve warm.

Mixed Fruit

Hints

Most fruit is best when in season in your area. This may affect your choice. You can also vary this recipe depending on your personal preferences or the dietary requirements of your guests. Here are a few examples to get you started.

Notes

Ingredients

Option A	Serves 6	Serves 12	Serves 24
Strawberries *(cut)*	8 ounces	16 ounces	32 ounces
Blackberries	6 ounces	12 ounces	24 ounces
Blueberries	6 ounces	12 ounces	24 ounces

Option B	Serves 6	Serves 12	Serves 24
Fresh Pitted Cherries	8 ounces	16 ounces	32 ounces
Oranges *(sliced)*	2	4	8

Option C	Serves 6	Serves 12	Serves 24
Peaches *(peeled, sliced)*	3	6	12
Blueberries or Raspberries	8 ounces	16 ounces	32 ounces

Option D	Serves 6	Serves 12	Serves 24
Grapes *(halved)*	8 ounces	16 ounces	32 ounces
Melon *(peeled, sliced, cut into 1" cubes)*	12 ounces	24 ounces	48 ounces
Kiwi *(peeled, sliced)*	1	2	3

Method

1. Rinse fruit and drain well in a colander.
2. Prepare any fruit that needs to be peeled, cut, or sliced.
3. Keep fruit separate and add to plates as garnish. Or add all fruit to a mixing bowl and stir gently to combine.
4. Refrigerate until ready to serve.

Menu Timeline

Prep Actions	Timing

Prep Actions   **Timing**

1. Verify your supply of ingredients. Purchase any items needed to complete all recipes. Bacon can be frozen until ready to prepare.

2. Banana Walnut Muffins can be prepared the day before serving. You may also prepare up to 1 month ahead and store in an airtight container in the freezer. Let the muffins cool completely before storing.

3. Cinnamon Butter can be prepared ahead and stored in the refrigerator for several weeks.

1+
days

1. Remove bacon *(2 to 3 slices per guest)* from freezer. Place in the refrigerator to thaw overnight.

2. Prepare muffins according to recipe. If these were previously prepared and frozen, remove muffins *(1 per guest)* from the freezer. Place muffins in an airtight container on the counter.

3. Prepare cinnamon butter if this was not done previously.

4. Check that your table linens are fresh and clean if you are using these. Set the table adding napkins, flatware, juice glasses, and coffee mugs. Add a selection of sweeteners in a dish, as well as salt and pepper shakers.

5. Run the dishwasher so you begin tomorrow with clean dishes and an empty dishwasher ready for all of the breakfast dishes.

24+
hours

1. Turn on coffee maker. Turn on lights and music for a nice atmosphere for the cook and the guests.

2. Remove cinnamon butter from the refrigerator to soften.

3. Place muffins on a baking sheet lined with parchment paper and cover with foil.

4. Thaw bacon if this was not done the day before.

2
hours

Menu Timeline

Timing	Prep Actions

Timing

Prep Actions

1 **45**
hour   min

1. Place raisin bread on a baking sheet lined with parchment paper. Plan on 1 slice per guest. Unless you want some extras!

2. Pour juices and water into pitchers. Keep in the refrigerator until serving.

3. Set the table if this was not done the day before.

4. Empty clean dishes from the dishwasher.

5. Make a pot of coffee for the cook and early risers.

1 **30**
hour   min

1. Fill 3 small bowls with oatmeal toppings, 1 each for chopped walnuts, craisins, and brown sugar. Add a spoon to each bowl.

2. Wash and prepare the Mixed Fruit option of your choice. Refrigerate until serving.

3. Take a moment to put away the ingredients you have finished using. Put used dishes and utensils into the dishwasher.

1
hour

1. Preheat the oven to 350°F.

2. Start water boiling for the oatmeal. You might want to add just a tad more water, especially if you are cooking with gas. This will allow for evaporation and keep the oatmeal from becoming too dry.

3. Prepare oatmeal according to recipe.

4. Set out the plates. Add a small napkin or washable coaster to the plate for the individual dishes. This keeps the dish from slipping on the plate and protects from the very hot dishes.

Menu Timeline

Prep Actions	Timing
1. Cook bacon slices according to the package directions. Cook slices steadily at medium heat (do not have the heat too high), turning every few minutes until bacon reaches desired crispness. HINT: Remove the bacon a bit before it reaches the desired crispness. Bacon will continue to cook for a few minutes after removed from the heat and turn out perfectly. 2. Place the bacon on a small baking sheet between layers of paper towels. Cover with foil to keep warm.	**45** min
1. Place muffins in the oven for 5 to 7 minutes to warm. To avoid overheating, set a timer for 7 minutes. 2. Prepare egg mixture to scramble. 3. Remove muffins from oven.	**30** min
1. Spread the raisin bread with prepared cinnamon butter. 2. Bake at 350°F until bubbly on top, about 5 to 10 minutes. Keep a close watch on this! 3. Prepare oven safe dishes with nonstick cooking spray.	**20** min
1. Fill oven safe dishes with servings of oatmeal. Take care not to fill all the way to the top as oatmeal will be a bit bubbly while baking. Place dishes on a baking sheet for easier handling. 2. Generously sprinkle raw sugar over the top of the oatmeal. 3. Place juices, water, and creamer on the table.	**15** min

Menu Timeline

Timing	Prep Actions
10 min	1. Remove cinnamon toast from oven. 2. Increase the oven temperature to Broil (500°F). 3. Scramble the eggs and divide cooked eggs among each plate. 4. Place the dishes of oatmeal on a baking sheet and place under broiler until sugar is bubbly. Watch carefully, this will only take 2 to 5 minutes. Remove from oven. 5. Carefully place a dish of oatmeal on a napkin or coaster on each plate. 6. Add a muffin, 2 slices of bacon, and a serving of mixed fruit to the plates. 7. Place toast under broiler 1 to 2 minutes. Watch carefully! Remove from oven. Slice diagonally and add 2 halves to each plate.
0 ready	1. Serve each guest a beautiful plate. 2. Offer coffee or tea.

MENU

Red Pepper Casserole
Herb and Cheddar Scones
Apricot Pecan Granola with Yogurt
White Cheddar Grits

Red Pepper Casserole

Ingredients

	Serves 8	Serves 16	Serves 24
Crescent Rolls (*tube of 8*)	1 can	2 cans	3 cans
Bulk Sausage (*crumbled, cooked, drained*)	1 pound	2 pounds	3 pounds
Mozzarella Cheese (*shredded*)	1 cup	2 cups	3 cups
Sharp Cheddar Cheese (*shredded*)	1 cup	2 cups	3 cups
Eggs	5	10	15
Milk	¾ cup	1½ cups	2¼ cups
Salt	½ teaspoon	1 teaspoon	1½ teaspoons
Pepper	½ teaspoon	1 teaspoon	1½ teaspoons
Red Bell Pepper (*julienned*)	¾ cup	1½ cups	2¼ cups

Hints

One 9 x 13 baking dish is needed per 8 servings.

This casserole also works with fresh tomato on top (sliced thin or diced small), instead of or in addition to the fresh red bell pepper.

Notes

Method

1. Preheat the oven to 400°F. Prepare a 9 x 13 baking dish with butter or nonstick cooking spray.

2. Roll out crescent rolls and place flat to line the bottom of prepared dish, pinching the seams together so there are no gaps.

3. In a large skillet, crumble sausage and cook throughly. Drain fat.

4. Spread the cooked sausage on top of the pastry. Sprinkle both cheeses over the sausage.

5. Using a whisk, mix the eggs, milk, salt, and pepper in a medium bowl. Pour mixture over the sausage and cheeses.

6. Place julienned red bell pepper strips evenly over the egg mixture.

7. Bake at 400°F for 15 to 20 minutes. Casserole will be firm and golden brown when done. Let stand for 5 minutes before cutting.

Herb and Cheddar Scones

The dry and wet ingredients should be mixed together only until just combined. Overmixing the batter will result in baked scones with a tough texture.

Notes

Ingredients

	Makes 8	Makes 16	Makes 24
All Purpose Flour	2 cups	4 cups	6 cups
Sugar	1 Tablespoon	2 Tablespoons	3 Tablespoons
Baking Powder	1 teaspoon	2 teaspoons	1 Tablespoon
Baking Soda	¼ teaspoon	½ teaspoon	¾ teaspoon
Salt	½ teaspoon	1 teaspoon	1½ teaspoons
Black Pepper	¼ teaspoon	½ teaspoon	¾ teaspoon
Thyme	½ teaspoon	1 teaspoon	1½ teaspoons
Butter	4 ounces (*1 stick*)	8 ounces (*2 sticks*)	12 ounces (*3 sticks*)
Sharp Cheddar Cheese (*shredded*)	1 cup	2 cups	3 cups
Scallions (*chopped*)	⅓ cup	⅔ cup	1 cup
Sour Cream	½ cup	1 cup	1½ cups
Eggs	1	2	3

Method

1. Preheat oven to 400°F. Line a baking sheet with parchment paper.
2. Using a whisk, mix flour, sugar, baking powder, baking soda, salt, pepper, and thyme in a large bowl until well combined.
3. Slice the butter into tablespoon-size pieces and add to the flour mixture.
4. Using a pastry cutter, cut the butter pieces into the dry ingredients until the butter is pea-size.
5. Add shredded cheese and chopped scallions to the flour mixture and combine.
6. In a medium mixing bowl, stir together sour cream and egg(s). Add to the flour mixture and combine.
7. Let the dough rest for 10 minutes.

8. Turn out the dough onto a lightly floured surface. Shape into a circle and roll out to about ½ inch thick.

9. Cut the dough circle into 8 pie-shaped wedges and place on prepared baking sheet.

10. Bake at 400°F for 15 to 17 minutes. Rotate the baking sheet back to front at 7 minutes for even baking. Scones will appear slightly moist and very light brown when done.

11. Let the scones cool for 10 minutes before serving.

12. The scones can be prepared the day before serving. You may also prepare up to 1 month ahead and store in an airtight container in the freezer. Let the scones cool completely before storing.

Notes

Apricot Pecan Granola

Hints

Granola can be frozen in an airtight container for 1 month. Thaw before serving.

Notes

Ingredients

	Makes 3 Cups	Makes 6 Cups	Makes 9 Cups
Old-Fashioned Oats	2 cups	4 cups	6 cups
Unsweetened Shredded Coconut	½ cup	1 cup	1½ cups
Pecans	½ cup	1 cup	1½ cups
Brown Sugar *(packed)*	2 Tablespoons	4 Tablespoons	6 Tablespoons
Cinnamon	½ teaspoon	1 teaspoon	1½ teaspoons
Salt	¼ teaspoon	½ teaspoon	¾ teaspoon
Coconut Oil	¼ cup	½ cup	¾ cup
Maple Syrup	½ cup	1 cup	1½ cups
Vanilla Extract	½ teaspoon	1 teaspoon	1½ teaspoons
Dried Apricots	½ cup	1 cup	1½ cups

Method

1. Preheat oven to 300°F. Line a baking sheet with parchment paper.

2. In a large bowl, mix the oats, coconut, pecans, brown sugar, cinnamon, and salt together.

3. In a small saucepan, heat the coconut oil until melted. Remove from heat. Add the maple syrup and vanilla extract to the coconut oil, and mix well.

4. Pour the coconut oil mixture over the oat mixture and combine well to coat uniformly.

5. Spread the oat mixture evenly over prepared baking sheet.

6. Bake at 350°F for 30 minutes. Stir every 10 minutes. The mixture will be deep golden brown when done. Granola will not be crunchy until it has cooled for at least 20 minutes.

7. Once cooled completely, stir in the dried apricots.

8. Store in an airtight container. Enjoy!

White Cheddar Grits

Ingredients

	Serves 8	Serves 16	Serves 32
Water	3 cups	6 cups	12 cups
Salt	½ teaspoon	1 teaspoon	2 teaspoons
White Pepper	¼ teaspoon	½ teaspoon	1 teaspoon
Half & Half	1 cup	2 cups	4 cups
Quick Grits	1 cup	2 cups	4 cups
White Cheddar Cheese (*shredded*)	1 cup	2 cups	4 cups
Butter	2 Tablespoons	4 Tablespoons	8 Tablespoons
Garnish			
Cherry Tomatoes (*diced or quartered*)	8	16	32

Hints

Grits can pop and splatter while cooking. Use a pot large enough to have 2 to 3 inches of space above the cooking grits. This helps keep them in the pot and off your stovetop!

Notes

Method

1. Place water and salt into a large pot and bring to a boil.

2. Whisk in the grits slowly making sure to incorporate them fully into the liquid.

3. Reduce heat and cook until thick. Whisk often to ensure there are no lumps.

4. Add half & half, cheese, pepper, and butter to the grits. Stir until melted and incorporated.

5. Remove from heat and serve this delicious treat in individual bowls or 4 ounce ramekins (*~ ½ cup per guest*).

6. Garnish each serving with cherry tomato quarters in a flower pattern or sprinkle with diced tomatoes.

Menu Timeline

Timing	Prep Actions
1+ days	1. Verify your supply of ingredients. Purchase any items needed to complete each recipe. Bulk sausage can be frozen until ready to prepare. Plan for ⅓ cup of vanilla yogurt per guest to serve with the granola. Have a little fresh fruit on hand if you would like to add as a garnish to the plate. 2. Scones and granola can be prepared up to 1 month ahead and frozen in airtight containers. *(See recipes for storage instructions.)*
24+ hours	1. Remove the appropriate amount of bulk sausage from freezer for your number of guests. Place in refrigerator to thaw overnight. 2. Prepare scones and granola according to each recipe. If these were previously prepared, remove scones *(1 per guest)* and granola *(~ ⅓ cup per guest)* from the freezer. Place these in airtight containers on the counter. 3. Shred cheeses according to each recipe for the number of servings needed. For example, shred 1 cup Mozzarella cheese and 1 cup of sharp cheddar cheese for 8 servings of Red Pepper Casserole. 4. Julienne *(cut very thin strips)* of red bell pepper. 5. Check that your table linens are fresh and clean, if you are using these. Set the table adding napkins, flatware, juice glasses, and coffee mugs. Add sweeteners and salt and pepper shakers. 6. Run the dishwasher so you begin tomorrow with clean dishes and an empty dishwasher ready for the breakfast dishes.
2 hours	1. Turn on coffee maker. Turn on lights and music for a nice atmosphere for the cook and the guests. 2. Shred cheeses if this was not done the day before. Thaw sausage if this was not done the day before. 3. Place the scones on a baking sheet lined with parchment paper and cover with foil.

Menu Timeline

Prep Actions

	Timing

1. Pour juices and water into pitchers. Keep in the refrigerator until serving.
2. Set the table if this was not done the day before.
3. Empty clean dishes from the dishwasher.
4. Make a pot of coffee for the cook and early risers.

1 hour   **45** min

---

1. In a large skillet, crumble sausage and cook throughly. Drain fat.
2. While the sausage is cooking, prepare the egg mixture for the red pepper casserole following the recipe.
3. Prepare a 9 x 13 baking dish with nonstick cooking spray. Unroll the crescent roll dough and line the dish pinching together the seams.

1 hour   **30** min

---

1. Preheat oven to 400°F.
2. Dice or quarter cherry tomatoes for a garnish for the grits.
3. Prepare a small individual bowl for each guest with a ⅓ cup of vanilla yogurt on the bottom. Top the yogurt with a ⅓ cup of granola. Keep these in the refrigerator until ready to serve.

1 hour   **15** min

---

1. Prepare the grits according to the recipe.
2. Set out the plates.
3. Finish preparing the casserole according to the recipe.

45 min

---

1. Place casserole in the oven.
2. Take a moment to put away the ingredients you have finished using. Put used dishes and utensils into the dishwasher.

30 min

Menu Timeline

Timing	Prep Actions
20 min	1. Rotate the casserole from back to front in the oven for even baking. 2. Place scones in 400°F oven for 3 to 4 minutes to warm. To avoid overheating, set a timer for 4 minutes. 3. Remove scones from oven.
10 min	1. Place juices, water, and creamer on the table. 2. Place a bowl of yogurt and granola on the table above the fork at each place setting.
5 min	1. Remove casserole from oven. Let rest 5 minutes. Cut the casserole into 8 servings. 2. Scoop servings of grits into small ramekins. Top with the cherry tomatoes *(quartered or diced)*. 3. Add a serving of the casserole, grits, and a scone to each plate. Garnish with fresh fruit if you choose.
0 ready	1. Serve each guest a beautiful plate. 2. Offer coffee or tea.

MENU

Country Skillet
Biscuits with Apple Butter or Jam
Cranberry Orange Muffins

Country Skillet

Ingredients

	Serves 6	Serves 12	Serves 24
Bacon	1 pound	2 pounds	4 pounds
Onion (small diced)	¾ cup	1½ cups	3 cups
Shredded Frozen Hash Browns (thawed)	1 (30-ounce) package	2 (30-ounce) packages	4 (30-ounce) packages
Salt	½ teaspoon	1 teaspoon	2 teaspoons
Pepper	¼ teaspoon	½ teaspoon	1 teaspoon
Eggs	6	12	24
Sharp Cheddar Cheese (shredded)	1 cup	2 cups	4 cups

Method

1. Preheat oven to 350°F. Oil 10 inch cast iron skillet or six 5 inch skillets for individual servings. Set aside.

2. Cut bacon into fine strips with kitchen scissors. Dice the onion.

3. In a large skillet, cook bacon for about 5 minutes on medium heat. Add onion and continue cooking until the onion is browned and the bacon is cooked to desired crispiness.

4. Drain off fat, reserving ¼ cup, ½ cup, or 1 cup bacon fat according to the number of servings being prepared. Wipe off any fat drippings from the skillet before returning it to the heat.

5. Add reserved fat back into the skillet and heat on high. Carefully add the hash browns to the hot bacon and onion mixture.

6. Gently fold the hash browns into the mixture. Smooth over the bottom of the skillet. Cook unstirred for 5 to 7 minutes on high heat.

7. Sprinkle potatoes with salt and pepper.

8. Once the underside of the potatoes are browned, flip them over with a spatula and brown on the other side.

Hints

We have pictured the Country Skillet without the cheese topping to give you an idea of how the egg wells work in the baking dish. You will not want to skip the delicious addition of the cheese when preparing these skillets.

One 10 inch skillet or six 5 inch skillets are needed per six servings. Skillets should be cast iron.

Notes

9. Remove from the heat. Spread the hash brown mixture into 10 inch oiled skillet or divide mixture evenly between six small 5 inch oiled skillets.

10. If using a 10 inch skillet, make 6 evenly spaced indentions *(wells)* in the hash brown mixture. If using small skillets, make 1 indention in the middle of the mixture in each skillet.

11. Add an egg to each well. *(Break each egg into a small bowl first to avoid getting shell fragments in the food.)*

12. Place individual skillets on a baking sheet for easier handling. Place baking sheet in the oven. The 10 inch skillet can go directly in the oven.

13. Bake at 350°F for 10 minutes or until the eggs are set to your preference. *(An additional 2 to 5 minutes may be needed for a harder yolk.)*

14. Once the eggs are done, remove skillets from the oven and sprinkle sharp cheddar cheese around the edge of the dish. Let the cheese melt, then serve.

Biscuits

Ingredients

	Makes 12	Makes 25	Makes 50
All Purpose Flour	1 cup	2 cups	4 cups
Baking Powder	1 teaspoon	2 teaspoons	4 teaspoons
Baking Soda	¼ teaspoon	½ teaspoon	1 teaspoon
Salt	¼ teaspoon	½ teaspoon	1 teaspoon
Salted Butter	3 Tablespoons	6 Tablespoons	12 Tablespoons
Sour Cream	½ cup	1 cup	2 cups
Milk	1½ Tablespoons	3 Tablespoons	⅓ cup
Basting			
Salted Butter *(melted)*	4 Tablespoons	8 Tablespoons	12 Tablespoons

Method

1. Preheat oven to 400°F. Line a baking sheet with parchment paper.

2. Using a whisk, mix the flour, baking powder, baking soda, and salt in a medium bowl until well combined.

3. Slice the butter into tablespoon-size pieces and add to the flour mixture.

4. Using a pastry cutter, cut butter pieces into the dry ingredients until the butter is pea-size.

5. Add sour cream and milk. Mix until incorporated. Let rest for 10 minutes.

6. Roll out dough to 1 inch thickness on a lightly floured surface.

7. Using a round cutter or small juice glass, cut dough into 2 inch circles. Place on prepared baking sheet.

8. Bake at 400°F on middle rack for 5 minutes. Remove from oven and baste *(brush)* tops with melted butter. Rotate the baking sheet back to front and place on top rack in oven to ensure a nicely browned biscuit top.

9. Bake for 5 to 7 more minutes. The edges will be golden brown when done and the middle will spring back when touched lightly.

Hints

You can freeze the raw biscuits after they are cut by placing them in a single layer on a baking sheet lined with parchment paper. Place in the freezer 2 hours. Do not stack baking sheets. Store the frozen biscuits in an airtight container or large zip freezer bag.

Serve biscuits with apple butter or jam and softened butter.

Notes

Cranberry Orange Muffins

Hints

The dry and wet ingredients should be mixed together only until just combined. Overmixing the batter will result in baked muffins with a tough texture.

A squeeze release scoop is handy for filling muffin pans. A ½ cup (#8) scoop fills a regular size muffin pan perfectly. There will be less mess too!

Any empty muffin wells may be half-filled with water to keep the pan from warping in a hot oven.

Notes

Ingredients

	Makes 12	Makes 24	Makes 36
All Purpose Flour	2 cups	4 cups	6 cups
Sugar	½ cup	1 cup	1½ cups
Baking Powder	1½ teaspoons	3 teaspoons	4½ teaspoons
Salt	½ teaspoon	1 teaspoon	1½ teaspoons
Eggs	1	2	3
Vegetable Oil	¼ cup	½ cup	¾ cup
Milk	¾ cup	1½ cups	2¼ cups
Orange Juice	½ cup	1 cup	1½ cups
Orange Zest	1 teaspoon	2 teaspoons	1 Tablespoon
Dried Cranberries	¾ cup	1½ cups	2¼ cups
Topping			
Pecans *(chopped)*	¼ cup	½ cup	¾ cup
Brown Sugar *(packed)*	¼ cup	½ cup	¾ cup
Cinnamon	½ teaspoon	1 teaspoon	1½ teaspoons

Method

1. Preheat oven to 375°F. Prepare muffin pans with nonstick baking spray or paper liners.

2. In a small mixing bowl, combine chopped pecans, brown sugar, and cinnamon. Set aside.

3. Using a whisk, mix flour, sugar, baking powder, and salt in a large mixing bowl until well combined.

4. In a medium mixing bowl, beat egg(s) with a fork. Add oil, milk, orange juice, and orange zest and mix together.

5. Add egg mixture to flour mixture and mix until just combined.

6. Fold in dried cranberries.

7. Scoop batter into prepared muffin pans and sprinkle with pecan topping.

8. Bake 375°F for 12 to 15 minutes or until lightly golden brown. The center of the muffin will spring back with a gentle press to the top when done.

9. The muffins can be prepared the day before serving. You may also prepare up to 1 month ahead and store in an airtight container in the freezer. Let muffins cool completely before storing.

Notes

Menu Timeline

Timing	Prep Actions
1+ days	1. Verify your supply of ingredients. Purchase any items needed to complete each recipe. Bacon can be frozen until ready to prepare. Remember to have some apple butter or jam on hand for the biscuits. 2. It is helpful to have the Biscuits prepared ahead. Prepare and freeze unbaked biscuits according to the recipe up to 1 month before baking. 3. Cranberry Orange Muffins can be prepared, baked, and frozen up to 1 month.
24+ hours	1. Remove bacon from freezer. Place in the refrigerator to thaw overnight. 2. Prepare muffins and biscuits according to each recipe. If these were previously prepared and frozen, remove muffins *(1 per guest)* and biscuits *(1 per guest)* from the freezer. Place in airtight containers on the counter. 3. Grate cheese according to the recipe for the number of servings needed. For example, grate 1 cup sharp cheddar cheese for up to 6 servings. 4. Check that your table linens are fresh and clean if you are using these. Set the table adding napkins, flatware, juice glasses, and coffee mugs. Add a selection of sweeteners in a dish, as well as salt and pepper shakers. 5. Run the dishwasher so you begin tomorrow with clean dishes and an empty dishwasher ready for all of the breakfast dishes.

Menu Timeline

Prep Actions

Timing

1. Turn on coffee maker. Turn on lights and music for a nice atmosphere for the cook and the guests.
2. Shred cheese if this was not done the day before.
3. Remove bacon from the freezer to thaw if this was not done the day before.
4. Place muffins on a baking sheet lined with parchment paper and cover with foil.

2 hours

1. Pour juices and water into pitchers. Keep in the refrigerator until serving.
2. Set the table if this was not done the day before.
3. Empty clean dishes from the dishwasher.
4. Make a pot of coffee for the cook and early risers.

1 hour 45 min

1. Chop bacon and onion per recipe and cook together in a large skillet.
2. Remove hash browns from the freezer.

1 hour 30 min

1. Drain off ½ to ¾ cup of the excess fat from the onion and bacon.
2. Prepare individual cast iron skillets or 10 inch cast iron skillet with oil.

1 hour 15 min

Menu Timeline

Timing	Prep Actions
1 hour	1. Preheat oven to 350°F. 2. Add hash browns to the bacon and onion mixture. Cook in the reserved bacon fat according to the recipe. 3. Put apple butter or jam into a dish and place on the table. Add a butter dish to the table as well.
45 min	1. Set out the plates. 2. Add a small napkin or washable coaster to each plate if using the 5 inch skillets. This will help protect the plate from the very hot skillet.
30 min	1. Spoon hash brown, bacon, and onion mixture evenly into individual skillets. Using the back of a large spoon, make a "well" in the middle of each small skillet or 1 well per guest in the large skillet (for example, 6 wells for 6 guests). 2. Place muffins in the oven for 5 to 7 minutes to warm. To avoid overheating, set timer for 7 minutes. 3. Remove muffins from the oven.
20 min	1. Break 1 egg into each indentation for each serving. Place skillets in the oven. Bake for 10 minutes or until eggs are set. 2. Place biscuits in the oven for 5 minutes.

Menu Timeline

Prep Actions	**Timing**

1. Remove biscuits from the oven and brush tops with melted butter. Rotate the baking sheet back to front and move to the top rack for 5 to 7 minutes until biscuits are golden brown.

2. Take a moment to put away the ingredients you have finished using. Put used dishes and utensils into the dishwasher.

15
min

1. Place juices, water, and creamer on the table.

2. Remove the skillets from the oven when eggs are set to your liking *(an additional 2 to 5 minutes may be needed for a harder yoke)*. Immediately add cheddar cheese to the top.

10
min

1. Remove the biscuits from the oven.

2. Add a muffin and a biscuit to each plate. Or place these in a towel-lined breadbasket or bowl and place on the table.

5
min

1. Serve each guest a beautiful plate. Let them know the skillets are just from the oven and very hot.

2. Offer coffee or tea.

0
ready

MENU

Breakfast Burritos

Honey Cornmeal Scones
with Honey Butter

White Cheddar Grits

Orange Muffins
with Brown Sugar Glaze

Melon

Breakfast Burritos

Ingredients

	Makes 18	Makes 36	Makes 72
Butter	2 Tablespoons	4 Tablespoons	8 Tablespoons
Shredded Hash Browns *(frozen)*	½ (30-ounce) package	1 (30-ounce) package	2 (30-ounce) packages
Salt	½ teaspoon	1 teaspoon	2 teaspoons
Bulk Sausage *(crumbled, cooked, drained)*	1 pound	2 pounds	4 pounds
Bell Pepper *(any color, diced)*	¾ cup	1½ cups	3 cups
Onion *(diced)*	¼ cup + 2 Tablespoons	¾ cup	1½ cups
Eggs	12	24	48
Half & Half	¼ cup	½ cup	1 cup
Salt	¼ teaspoon	½ teaspoon	1 teaspoon
Pepper	¼ teaspoon	½ teaspoon	1 teaspoon
Sharp Cheddar Cheese *(shredded)*	2 cups	4 cups	8 cups
8″ Flour Tortilla Wraps *(uncooked)*	18	36	72
Garnish			
Sharp Cheddar Cheese *(shredded)*	½ cup	1 cup	2 cups

Hints

These can be made in large batches and frozen up to 2 months.

Garnish with diced tomatoes and cilantro.

Serve with salsa and sour cream.

Notes

Method

1. In a large skillet, heat butter on medium and cook hash browns according to package directions. Sprinkle with first measurement of salt. Place cooked hash browns in a large mixing bowl and set aside.

2. In the same skillet, crumble sausage and cook thoroughly. Drain off and reserve the fat. Add sausage to the bowl with hash browns.

3. Sauté the peppers and onion in a small amount of fat left over from the sausage. Set aside to cool slightly. Discard remaining fat.

4. While the peppers and onions are cooking, whisk together the eggs and half & half in a medium mixing bowl. Add the pepper and second measurement of salt to egg mixture, and stir.

5. Once the vegetables are translucent, add the egg mixture to the hot pan and cook thoroughly, stirring often. The mixture will have the consistency of scrambled eggs. (See recipe for scrambled eggs.)

6. Shred cheese and set aside.

7. Add the scrambled egg mixture and cheese to the sausage and hash browns in the large mixing bowl. Mix well.

8. In a large clean skillet, cook the tortilla wraps according to package directions.

9. Once cooked and while still warm, place a tortilla wrap on a pre-cut piece of waxed paper approximately 10 x 10.

10. Place ¼ cup of filling left of center on the tortilla wrap. Roll the small side of the wrap over the filling and tuck in both ends. Continue rolling the wrap until it is burrito shaped.

11. Roll waxed paper over the burrito in the same fashion. Place in an airtight container and freeze.

To Serve

1. The day before serving, unwrap burritos and place in baking dish seam side down. Cover with foil and place in refrigerator. Thaw overnight.

2. Preheat oven to 325°F.

3. Take burritos out of the refrigerator and place on the counter so the dishes can come to room temperature. Allowing the dishes to come to room temperature will help prevent them from breaking when placed in a hot oven.

4. Place burritos in the oven. Set timer for 15 minutes.

5. Remove burritos from the oven. Turn them seam side up. Re-cover dish with foil and return to the oven. Set timer for 15 minutes.

6. Remove burritos from the oven. Turn seam side down, top with shredded cheddar cheese. Return to the oven without foil for 5 minutes for cheese to melt.

7. Remove burritos from the oven. Garnish top of burritos with a sprinkling of tomatoes and cilantro.

Honey Cornmeal Scones

Ingredients

	Makes 12	Makes 24	Makes 36
All Purpose Flour	1½ cups	3 cups	4½ cups
Baking Powder	2 teaspoons	4 teaspoons	2 Tablespoons
Yellow Cornmeal	¾ cup	1½ cups	2¼ cups
Salt	¼ teaspoon	½ teaspoon	¾ teaspoon
Brown Sugar *(packed)*	¼ cup	½ cup	¾ cup
Butter	4 ounces (1 stick)	8 ounces (2 sticks)	12 ounces (3 sticks)
Eggs	1	2	3
Milk	½ cup	1 cup	1½ cups
Honey	¼ cup	½ cup	¾ cup
Vanilla Extract	½ teaspoon	1 teaspoon	1½ teaspoons

Method

1. Preheat oven to 375°F. Line a baking sheet with parchment paper.

2. Using a whisk, mix flour, baking powder, cornmeal, salt, and brown sugar in a large mixing bowl until well combined.

3. Slice butter into tablespoon-size pieces and add to the flour mixture. Using a pastry cutter, cut the butter pieces into the dry ingredients until the butter is pea-size.

4. Whisk egg(s) in a medium mixing bowl. Add milk, honey, and vanilla extract and whisk to combine.

5. Add the egg mixture to the flour mixture and mix until just combined.

6. Use a ½ cup (#8) scoop to portion out the batter into soft mounds on prepared baking sheet.

7. Bake at 375°F for 10 to 14 minutes until scones are just golden brown and firm to the touch.

Hints

The dry and wet ingredients should be mixed together only until just combined. Overmixing the batter will result in baked scones with a tough texture.

The scones can be prepared the day before serving. You may also prepare up to 1 month ahead and store in an airtight container in the freezer. Let the scones cool completely before storing.

Notes

Honey Butter

Ingredients

	Makes ¾ Cup	Makes 1½ Cups	Makes 2¼ Cups
Unsalted Butter (room temperature)	4 ounces (1 stick)	8 ounces (2 sticks)	12 ounces (3 sticks)
Honey	¼ cup	½ cup	¾ cup

Method

1. Place all ingredients in a mixing bowl. Using a hand mixer, mix until well combined.

2. Scrape down the sides of the bowl several times with a spatula while mixing to incorporate all the butter.

3. Honey butter can be prepared ahead and stored in an airtight container in the refrigerator for 1 month. Soften before using.

White Cheddar Grits

Ingredients

	Serves 8	Serves 16	Serves 32
Water	3 cups	6 cups	12 cups
Salt	½ teaspoon	1 teaspoon	2 teaspoons
Quick Grits	1 cup	2 cups	4 cups
Half & Half	1 cup	2 cups	4 cups
White Cheddar Cheese (*shredded*)	1 cup	2 cups	4 cups
White Pepper	¼ teaspoon	½ teaspoon	1 teaspoon
Butter	2 Tablespoons	4 Tablespoons	8 Tablespoons
Garnish			
Cherry Tomatoes (*diced*)	8	16	32
Cilantro (*chopped*)	2 Tablespoons	4 Tablespoons	8 Tablespoons

Hints

Grits can pop and splatter while cooking. Use a pot large enough to have 2 to 3 inches of space above the cooking grits. This helps keep them in the pot and off your stovetop!

Notes

Method

1. Place water and salt into a large pot and bring to a boil.

2. Whisk in the grits slowly making sure to incorporate them fully into the liquid.

3. Reduce heat and cook until thick. Whisk often to ensure there are no lumps.

4. Add half & half, cheese, pepper, and butter to the grits. Stir until melted and incorporated.

5. Remove from heat and serve this delicious treat in individual bowls or 4 ounce ramekins (~ ½ *cup per guest*).

6. Garnish each serving with diced tomatoes and chopped cilantro.

Orange Muffins with Brown Sugar Glaze

Hints

The dry and wet ingredients should be mixed together only until just combined. Overmixing the batter will result in baked muffins with a tough texture.

A squeeze release scoop is handy for filling muffin pans. A ½ cup (#8) scoop fills a regular size muffin pan perfectly. There will be less mess too!

Any empty muffin wells may be half-filled with water to keep the pan from warping in a hot oven.

Notes

Ingredients

	Makes 10	Makes 20	Makes 30
Butter	4 ounces (1 stick)	8 ounces (2 sticks)	12 ounces (3 sticks)
Sugar	½ cup	1 cup	1½ cups
All Purpose Flour	1 cup	2 cups	3 cups
Salt	¼ teaspoon	½ teaspoon	¾ teaspoon
Eggs	1	2	3
Buttermilk	½ cup	1 cup	1½ cups
Baking Soda	½ teaspoon	1 teaspoon	1½ teaspoons
Glaze			
Oranges (zested, juiced)	1	2	3
Brown Sugar (packed)	½ cup	1 cup	1½ cups

Method

1. Preheat oven to 350°F. Prepare muffin pans with nonstick baking spray or paper liners.

2. Zest and juice the orange(s) keeping the zest separate from the juice. Set both aside.

3. Using a hand mixer, cream the butter and sugar in a large mixing bowl. Add in the egg(s) one at a time. Beat after each egg is added until mixture is light and fluffy.

4. Dissolve the baking soda into the buttermilk and set aside.

5. Using a whisk, mix flour, salt, and orange zest in a medium mixing bowl until well combined. Stir the flour mixture into the butter mixture.

6. Add the buttermilk mixture to the flour and butter mixture. Stir until all ingredients are just combined.

7. Scoop batter into prepared muffin pans.

8. Bake at 350°F for 15 to 18 minutes or until lightly brown. The center of the muffin will spring back with a gentle press to the top when done.

9. Let muffins cool slightly before removing from pan.

10. The muffins can be prepared the day before serving. You may also prepare up to 1 month ahead and store in an airtight container in the freezer. Let the muffins cool completely before storing.

11. While the muffins are baking, combine orange juice and brown sugar.

12. Pour the brown sugar glaze over the warm muffins and let that goodness soak in.

Notes

Menu Timeline

Timing	Prep Actions

Timing

Prep Actions

1+
days

1. Verify your supply of ingredients. Purchase any items needed to complete each recipe. Plan for melon slices and tomato and cilantro garnish for the burritos.
2. Honey Cornmeal Scones and Orange Muffins can be prepared the day before serving. You may also prepare up to 1 month ahead and store in an airtight container in the freezer. Let the scones and muffins cool completely before storing. Brown Sugar Glaze for the Orange Muffins should be reserved until the muffins are warmed prior to serving.
3. Honey Butter can be prepared ahead and refrigerated for 1 month.

24+
hours

1. Remove Breakfast Burritos (*2 per guest*) from the freezer. Place these in an airtight container in the refrigerator.
2. Prepare scones and muffins according to each recipe. If these were previously prepared and frozen, remove scones (*1 per guest*) and muffins (*1 per guest*) from the freezer. Place these in an airtight container on the counter.
3. Shred cheeses according to each recipe for the number of servings needed. For example, shred 1 cup white cheddar for 8 servings of grits and ½ cup sharp cheddar for garnish on 9 servings of burritos.
4. Check that your table linens are fresh and clean if you are using these. Set the table adding napkins, flatware, juice glasses, and coffee mugs. Add a selection of sweeteners in a dish, as well salt and pepper shakers.

2
hours

1. Turn on coffee maker. Turn on lights and music for a nice atmosphere for the cook and the guests.
2. Take honey butter out of refrigerator to soften.
3. Place scones and muffins on a baking sheet lined with parchment paper and cover with foil.
4. Remove burritos from the freezer to thaw if this was not done the day before.

Menu Timeline

Prep Actions	**Timing**

1. Pour juices and water into pitchers. Keep in the refrigerator until serving.
2. Set the table if this was not done the day before.
3. Empty clean dishes from the dishwasher.
4. Make a pot of coffee for the cook and early risers.

1 hour **45** min

1. Peel and slice melon. Refrigerate until plating.
2. Unwrap burritos and place in baking dish seam side down. Cover with foil.

1 hour **15** min

1. Preheat oven to 325°F.
2. Set out the plates.

1 hour

1. Place burritos in the oven. Set timer for 15 minutes.
2. Place honey butter on the table.
3. Dice tomato and chop cilantro for burrito garnish.
4. Take a moment to put away the ingredients you have finished using. Put used dishes and utensils into the dishwasher.

45 min

1. Prepare the White Cheddar Grits according to the recipe.
2. Remove burritos from oven. Turn them seam side up and cover pan with foil. Return to the oven. Set timer for 15 minutes.
3. Prepare brown sugar glaze.

30 min

Menu Timeline

Timing	Prep Actions

Timing

Prep Actions

15
min

1. Remove burritos from the oven. Turn seam side down, top with shredded cheddar cheese. Return to the oven without foil for 5 minutes for cheese to melt.
2. Place muffins and scones in the oven for 6 to 8 minutes to warm. To avoid overheating, set a timer for 8 minutes.
3. Add salsa and sour cream to small bowls and place on the table.
4. Place juices, water, and creamer on the table.
5. Remove muffins and scones from the oven.
6. Pour brown sugar glaze over the orange muffins.

10
min

1. Remove burritos from the oven.
2. Scoop grits into a ramekin or small bowl for each serving.
3. Prepare each plate with a serving of grits, 2 burritos, and melon slices. Garnish top of burritos with a sprinkling of tomatoes and cilantro.
4. Add a muffin and scone to each plate. Or place these in a towel-lined breadbasket or bowl and place on the table.

0
ready

1. Serve each guest a beautiful plate.
2. Offer coffee or tea.

MENU

Garden Quiche

Roasted Rosemary Sweet Potatoes

Ginger Pumpkin Muffins

Citrus Fruit Salad

Chicken Sausage

Tea Biscuits

Garden Quiche

Ingredients

	Serves 8	Serves 12	Serves 16
Butter	1 Tablespoon	1½ Tablespoons	2 Tablespoons
Zucchini (*grated*)	2 cups	3 cups	4 cups
Scallion (*chopped fine*)	½ cup	¾ cup	1 cup
Garlic (*minced*)	3 cloves	4 cloves	5 cloves
Eggs	8	12	16
Heavy Cream	½ cup	¾ cup	1 cup
Parmesan Cheese (*grated*)	½ cup	¾ cup	1 cup
Basil (*chopped*)	2 Tablespoons	3 Tablespoons	4 Tablespoons
Salt	½ teaspoon	¾ teaspoon	1 teaspoon
Pepper	¼ teaspoon	¼ teaspoon	½ teaspoon
Nutmeg	⅛ teaspoon	⅛ teaspoon	¼ teaspoon

Hints

This quiche can be frozen for 1 month after baking.

The zucchini mixture can be prepared ahead and refrigerated overnight or frozen for 1 month. Let cool before storing.

Notes

Method

1. Preheat oven to 375°F. Prepare individual 10 ounce oven safe dishes or 1 large pie or tart pan with nonstick baking spray. Individual dishes should be placed on a baking sheet for easier handling.

2. Prepare pie crust and place into prepared dish(es).

3. Grate zucchini. Chop scallions and garlic.

4. In a large skillet, heat butter on medium until bubbly. Add garlic and cook stirring often for 1 minute or until garlic is slightly golden.

5. Add zucchini and scallions to the hot skillet and cook for another 5 minutes. Remove from heat and set aside. (*Mixture can be frozen at this step. See Hints.*)

6. In a large bowl, mix eggs, heavy cream, Parmesan cheese, basil, salt, pepper, and nutmeg until well combined.

7. Distribute the zucchini mixture evenly in the prepared pie shells. Pour egg mixture evenly over zucchini mixture.

8. Bake at 375°F for 10 to 15 minutes for individual dishes, 20 to 25 minutes for a larger pie or tart pan. Quiche will be golden brown when done.

Pie Crust

Ingredients

	Makes 1 Large Tart or 8 Individual Tarts	Makes 2 Large Tarts or 12 Individual Tarts	Makes 3 Large Tarts or 16 Individual Tarts
All Purpose Flour	2 cups	3 cups	4 cups
Salt	½ teaspoon	¾ teaspoon	1 teaspoon
Shortening	1 cup	1½ cups	2 cups
Lemon Juice	1 Tablespoon	1½ Tablespoons	2 Tablespoons
Egg Yokes	2	3	4
Cold Water	7 to 8 Tablespoons	⅔ to ¾ cup	1 cup

Hints

Pinched for time? Use a prepared refrigerated pie crust sheet.

Notes

Method

1. Using a whisk, mix flour and salt in a large mixing bowl.

2. Add shortening to the flour mixture. Using a pastry cutter, cut shortening into the flour mixture until the shortening is pea-size.

3. Add lemon juice, egg yolks, and half of the water measurement to flour mixture.

4. Combine the ingredients, adding more water in small amounts to reach a pliable consistency.

5. Cover the bowl with a clean towel. Let the dough rest 10 minutes in the refrigerator.

6. Divide dough into even portions for individual tarts.

7. Sprinkle flour on a flat work surface and roll out the dough to ¼ inch thickness.

8. Place in 12 inch pie or tart pan, or individual 6 inch dishes. Press to smooth in the bottom and sides of the pan or dishes.

Roasted Rosemary Sweet Potatoes

Hints

Raw sweet potatoes are very hard. Take care when peeling and dicing.

Notes

Ingredients

	Serves 8	Serves 12	Serves 16
Sweet Potatoes	4 large	6 large	8 large
Olive oil	3 Tablespoons	¼ cup	⅓ cup
Salt	1 teaspoon	1½ teaspoons	2 teaspoons
Pepper	½ teaspoon	¾ teaspoon	1 teaspoon
Fresh Rosemary *(chopped)*	2 teaspoons	3 teaspoons	4 teaspoons

Method

1. Preheat oven to 375°F. Line a baking sheet with parchment paper.

2. Wash potatoes and pat dry.

3. Peel and small dice sweet potatoes. *(Approximately ½ sweet potato per guest. This will result in ¾ to 1 cup of potato cubes per guest.)*

4. In a large bowl, toss the diced potatoes with the olive oil, rosemary, salt, and pepper.

5. Evenly scatter the sweet potatoes over prepared baking sheet.

6. Bake at 375°F for 40 to 45 minutes. Stir potatoes and rotate baking sheet every 15 minutes.

Ginger Pumpkin Muffins

Ingredients

	Makes 14	Makes 30	Makes 45
Pecan Topping			
Sugar	1½ Tablespoons	3 Tablespoons	¼ cup
Ground Ginger	1 teaspoon	2 teaspoons	3 teaspoons
Salt	¼ teaspoon	½ teaspoon	¾ teaspoon
Egg White	2 teaspoons	1 Tablespoon	2 Tablespoons
Pecans (chopped)	¾ cup	1½ cups	2¼ cups
Batter			
Eggs	2	4	6
Sugar	1¼ cup	2½ cups	3¾ cups
Pumpkin Puree	¾ cup & 3 Tablespoons	1¾ cups	2⅔ cups
Vegetable Oil	½ cup	1 cup	1½ cups
Water	2 Tablespoons	4 Tablespoons	6 Tablespoons
Vanilla	1½ teaspoons	3 teaspoons	5 teaspoons
All Purpose Flour	1¾ cups	3½ cups	5¼ cups
Cinnamon	1 Tablespoon	2 Tablespoons	3 Tablespoons
Baking Soda	1 teaspoon	2 teaspoons	3 teaspoons
Salt	½ teaspoon	1 teaspoon	1½ teaspoons
Ground Ginger	½ teaspoon	1 teaspoon	1½ teaspoons
Nutmeg	¼ teaspoon	½ teaspoon	¾ teaspoon
Crystalized Ginger (chopped)	¼ cup	½ cup	¾ cup

Hints

The egg white for the topping can be taken from one egg in the batter ingredients.

The dry and wet ingredients should be mixed together only until just combined. Overmixing the batter will result in baked muffins with a tough texture.

A squeeze release scoop is handy for filling muffin pans. A ½ cup (#8) scoop fills a regular size muffin pan perfectly. There will be less mess too!

This recipe makes more batter than needed for a standard 12 cup muffin pan. You can add extra batter to a 6 cup muffin pan. Any empty muffin wells may be half-filled with water to keep the pan from warping in a hot oven.

Method

1. Preheat oven to 350°F. Prepare muffin pans with nonstick baking spray or paper liners. Line a baking sheet with parchment paper.

2. In a small bowl, combine the first measurement of sugar, ground ginger, salt, and egg white. Add chopped pecans and mix to coat.

Notes

3. Place the topping mixture on the prepared baking sheet. Bake at 350°F for 12 to 15 minutes, then let cool.

4. In a large mixing bowl, beat eggs and second measurement of sugar with a hand mixer until fluffy.

5. Add pumpkin puree, oil, water, and vanilla to the egg mixture. Mix until well incorporated. Set aside.

6. In a separate mixing bowl, mix flour, cinnamon, baking soda, salt, ground ginger, and nutmeg using a whisk until well combined.

7. Slowly add flour mixture to pumpkin mixture. Stir only until just combined.

8. Fold in crystallized ginger.

9. Scoop batter into prepared muffin pans. Sprinkle the top of each muffin with the prepared pecan topping.

10. Bake at 350°F for 25 to 30 minutes. The center of the muffin will spring back with a gentle press to the top when done.

11. The muffins can be prepared the day before serving. You may also prepare up to 1 month ahead and store in an airtight container in the freezer. Let the muffins cool completely before storing.

Tea Biscuits

Quick Biscuit Mix

	Makes 3 Cups	Makes 6 Cups	Makes 12 Cups
All Purpose Flour	2½ cups	5 cups	10 cups
Baking Powder	4½ teaspoons	3 Tablespoons	6 Tablespoons
Cornstarch	¼ cup	½ cup	1 cup
Sugar	1 Tablespoon	2 Tablespoons	¼ cup
Salt	½ teaspoon	1 teaspoon	2 teaspoons
Cold Butter	4 ounces (1 stick)	8 ounces (2 sticks)	16 ounces (4 sticks)

Method

1. Using a whisk, mix flour, baking powder, cornstarch, sugar, and salt in a large bowl until well combined.

2. Slice butter into tablespoon-size pieces and add to the flour mixture. Using a pastry cutter, cut butter pieces into the dry ingredients until the butter is tiny pea-size. Place in an airtight container and freeze for 2 months.

Tea Biscuits

	Makes 12	Makes 24	Makes 48
Butter	2 ounces (½ stick)	4 ounces (1 stick)	8 ounces (2 sticks)
Sour Cream	½ cup	1 cup	2 cups
Quick Biscuit Mix	1 cup	2 cups	4 cups

Method

1. Preheat oven to 375°F. Prepare mini muffin pan with nonstick baking spray. Melt butter.

2. In a medium mixing bowl, add biscuit mix, sour cream, and melted butter. Stir to incorporate all ingredients.

3. Scoop batter into prepared mini muffin pan.

4. Bake at 375°F for 8 to 10 minutes or until lightly golden brown.

Hints

Jam is nice to serve with these biscuits.

A squeeze release scoop is handy for filling muffin pans. A 2 Tablespoon (#40) scoop fills a mini size muffin pan perfectly. There is less mess too!

Purchased dry biscuit/pancake mix can be substituted for the Quick Biscuit Mix.

Notes

Citrus Fruit Salad

Notes

Ingredients

	Yield 6	Yield 12	Yield 24
Grapefruit	2	4	8
Naval Oranges	2	4	8
Cara Cara Blood Oranges	2	4	8
Coconut (shredded)	⅓ cup	⅔ cup	1⅓ cups

Method

1. Wash fruit and pat dry.

2. Peel and section fruit.

3. Add all fruit and coconut to a large mixing bowl. Fold gently to combine.

4. Refrigerate until ready to serve.

Menu Timeline

Prep Actions	Timing

Prep Actions

1. Verify your supply of ingredients. Purchase any items needed to complete each recipe. Chicken sausage links may be refrigerated or frozen until ready to prepare. Have some jam or apple butter on hand to serve with the tea biscuits.

2. Tea Biscuits and Ginger Pumpkin Muffins can be prepared the day before serving. You may also prepare up to 1 month ahead and store in an airtight container in the freezer. Let the tea biscuits and muffins cool completely before storing.

3. Garden Quiche can be frozen for 1 month after it has been prepared and baked. The zucchini mixture can be prepared ahead and frozen for 1 month.

1+
days

1. Remove chicken sausage *(1 per guest)* from the freezer. Place these in an airtight container in the refrigerator to thaw overnight.

2. Prepare muffins and tea biscuits according to each recipe. If these were previously prepared and frozen, remove muffins *(1 per guest)* and biscuits *(2 per guest)* from the freezer. Place these in airtight containers on the counter.

3. Prepare the zucchini mixture or remove frozen mixture from the freezer. Place in the refrigerator.

4. Prepare Pie Crust according to the recipe through step 5. Refrigerate overnight in a sealed bowl.

5. Check that your table linens are fresh and clean if you are using these. Set the table adding napkins, flatware, juice glasses, and coffee mugs. Add a selection of sweeteners in a dish, as well as salt and pepper shakers.

6. Run the dishwasher so you begin tomorrow with clean dishes and an empty dishwasher ready for all of the breakfast dishes.

24+
hours

Menu Timeline

Timing	Prep Actions

Timing

2 hours

1 hour **45** min

1 hour **15** min

1 hour

Prep Actions

2 hours

1. Turn on coffee maker. Turn on lights and music for a nice atmosphere for the cook and the guests.
2. Thaw sausages, muffins, and tea biscuits if this was not done the day before. Add muffins and tea biscuits to a baking sheet lined with parchment paper and cover with foil.
3. Make Citrus Fruit Salad according to the recipe and place in refrigerator until serving.

1 hour 45 min

1. Pour juices and water into pitchers. Keep in the refrigerator until serving.
2. Set the table if this was not done the day before.
3. Empty clean dishes from the dishwasher.
4. Make a pot of coffee for the cook and early risers.

1. Remove pie crust dough from the refrigerator. Place into a prepared pan or individual dishes according to the recipe.
2. Prepare the sweet potatoes according to the recipe. Spread potatoes over a baking sheet lined with parchment paper.

1 hour 15 min

1. Preheat oven to 375°F.
2. Remove prepared quiche mixture from the refrigerator. Add zucchini and egg mixtures to the prepared pie crust according to the recipe. Individual dishes should be placed on a baking sheet for easier handling.

1 hour

1. Place sweet potatoes in the oven.
2. In a large skillet, cook chicken sausages according to package directions. Place sausages in a small ovenproof dish. Cover with foil to keep warm.

Menu Timeline

Prep Actions	Timing

Prep Actions

1. If using one large pie dish, place the quiche in the oven.
2. Stir the sweet potatoes.

45 min

1. If using individual dishes, place quiches in the oven.
2. Rotate quiche from back to front for even baking if using large dish.
3. Stir the sweet potatoes.
4. Set out the plates. Add a small napkin or washable coaster to the plate if using individual dishes. This keeps the dish from slipping on the plate.

30 min

1. Rotate quiches back to front in the oven if using individual dishes.
2. Place juices, water, and creamer on the table.
3. Place a bowl of citrus fruit salad on the table above the fork at each place setting.

20 min

1. Remove potatoes and quiche from the oven.
2. Place muffins and tea biscuits in the oven for 3 to 4 minutes to warm. To avoid overheating, set a timer for 4 minutes. Remove muffins and biscuits from oven.
3. Prepare each plate with a serving of quiche, ½ to ¾ cup of potatoes, and a sausage link.
4. Add a muffin and biscuits to each plate. Or place these in a towel-lined breadbasket or bowl and place on the table.

10 min

1. Serve each guest a beautiful plate.
2. Offer coffee or tea.

0 ready

MENU

Farmhouse Breakfast Bowls
Carrot Raisin Muffins
Biscuits
Bacon
Mixed Fruit

Farmhouse Breakfast Bowls

Ingredients

	Serves 6	Serves 12	Serves 24
Russet Potatoes	3 medium	6 medium	12 medium
Olive Oil	3 Tablespoons	⅓ cup	⅔ cup
Salt and Pepper	to taste	to taste	to taste
Monterey Jack Cheese *(shredded)*	1 cup	2 cups	4 cups
Cream Cheese	8 ounces	16 ounces	32 ounces
Eggs	10	20	40
Salt and Pepper	to taste	to taste	to taste
Sharp Cheddar Cheese *(shredded)*	1 cup	2 cups	4 cups
Tomato Basil Compote			
Roma Tomatoes *(small diced)*	2	4	8
Fresh Basil *(chopped)*	1 Tablespoon	2 Tablespoons	¼ cup
Salt	dash	⅛ teaspoon	¼ teaspoon
Pepper	dash	⅛ teaspoon	¼ teaspoon

Hints

These bowls can be prepped the day before. Complete steps 1 to 7A. Preheat oven to 375°F before baking.

Notes

Method

1. Preheat oven to 400°F. Line a baking sheet with parchment paper.

2. Wash potatoes and pat dry. Dice potatoes and add to a large bowl. Toss with olive oil, salt, and pepper.

3. Evenly scatter potatoes over prepared baking sheet.

4. Bake at 400°F for 30 to 35 minutes until brown and crispy. Stir potatoes and rotate baking sheet every 10 minutes.

5. Lower the oven temperature to 375°F.

6. Prepare 10 ounce oven safe bowls with nonstick cooking spray. Layer bottom of each bowl with equal portion of the roasted potatoes. Prepare 1 bowl for each guest. Place dishes on a baking sheet for easier handling.

Notes

7. A. Cover the potatoes with equal portions of the shredded Monterey Jack cheese. *(If preparing the day before serving, allow bowls to cool, cover with plastic wrap, and store overnight in the refrigerator.)*
   B. Place bowls in the oven for 8 to 10 minutes to melt the cheese. *(If prepared the day before, remove the dishes from the refrigerator and allow them to come to room temperature before placing in the oven.)*

8. Place cream cheese in a bowl. Melt in the microwave until soft. Once melted, whisk in 1 egg per 8 ounces of cream cheese until mixture is a creamy consistency. Add the remaining eggs to the mixture and mix well. Season with salt and pepper.

9. Pour egg mixture evenly over the potatoes in each bowl. Top with cheddar cheese.

10. Bake at 375°F for 15 minutes, or until the egg mixture is firm.

11. Prepare the Tomato Basil Compote. Chop tomato and basil and combine with salt and pepper.

12. Place a generous spoonful of Tomato Basil Compote on top of each portion and serve.

Carrot Raisin Muffins

Ingredients

	Makes 10	Makes 20	Makes 30
All Purpose Flour	1 cup	2 cups	3 cups
Baking Powder	½ teaspoon	1 teaspoon	1½ teaspoons
Salt	½ teaspoon	1 teaspoon	1½ teaspoons
Baking Soda	¾ teaspoon	1½ teaspoons	2¼ teaspoons
Cinnamon	½ teaspoon	1 teaspoon	1½ teaspoons
Vegetable Oil	½ cup	1 cup	1½ cups
Sugar	⅔ cup	1⅓ cups	2 cups
Eggs	2	3	5
Molasses	2 Tablespoons	¼ cup	⅓ cup
Vanilla Extract	½ teaspoon	1 teaspoon	1½ teaspoons
Carrots (peeled, shredded)	½ cup	1 cup	1½ cups
Raisins	6 Tablespoons	¾ cup	1¼ cups
Walnuts (chopped)	6 Tablespoons	¾ cup	1¼ cups

Hints

The dry and wet ingredients should be mixed together only until just combined. Overmixing the batter will result in baked muffins with a tough texture.

A squeeze release scoop is handy for filling muffin pans. A ½ cup (#8) scoop fills a regular size muffin pan perfectly. There will be less mess too!

Any empty muffin wells may be half-filled with water to keep the pan from warping in a hot oven.

Notes

Method

1. Preheat oven to 350°F. Prepare muffin pans with nonstick baking spray or paper liners. Line a baking sheet with parchment paper.

2. Place walnuts on prepared baking sheet. Bake at 350°F for 5 to 7 minutes, then set aside. Set a timer as these can quickly burn.

3. Using a whisk, mix flour, baking powder, salt, baking soda, and cinnamon in a medium mixing bowl until well combined. Set aside.

4. In a large mixing bowl, combine the oil, sugar, eggs, molasses, and vanilla.

5. Add the flour mixture to the egg mixture and mix until just combined.

6. Add shredded carrots, raisins, and walnuts to the batter and gently fold together.

7. Scoop batter into prepared muffin pans.

8. Bake at 350°F for 25 to 35 minutes or until a toothpick inserted at the center comes out clean. The muffins will spring back from a gentle touch on the top when done.

9. The muffins can be prepared the day before serving. You may also prepare up to 1 month ahead and store in an airtight container in the freezer. Let muffins cool completely before storing.

Yogurt and Fruit Garnish

Notes

Ingredients

	Serves 10	Serves 20	Serves 30
Vanilla Yogurt or Plain Yogurt	5 teaspoons	¼ cup	⅓ cup
Strawberries	5	10	15
Blueberries	30	60	90

Method

1. Just before serving, add a dollop *(~ ½ teaspoon)* of vanilla or plain yogurt to the top of each muffin.

2. Place ½ strawberry and 3 blueberries on the yogurt as a garnish.

Biscuits

Ingredients

	Makes 12	Makes 25	Makes 50
All Purpose Flour	1 cup	2 cups	4 cups
Baking Powder	1 teaspoon	2 teaspoons	4 teaspoons
Baking Soda	¼ teaspoon	½ teaspoon	1 teaspoon
Salt	¼ teaspoon	½ teaspoon	1 teaspoon
Salted Butter	3 Tablespoons	6 Tablespoons	12 Tablespoons
Sour Cream	½ cup	1 cup	2 cups
Milk	1½ Tablespoons	3 Tablespoons	⅓ cup
Basting			
Salted Butter *(melted)*	4 Tablespoons	8 Tablespoons	12 Tablespoons

Method

1. Preheat oven to 400°F. Line a baking sheet with parchment paper.

2. Using a whisk, mix the flour, baking powder, baking soda, and salt in a medium bowl until well combined.

3. Slice the butter into tablespoon-size pieces and add to the flour mixture.

4. Using a pastry cutter, cut butter pieces into the dry ingredients until the butter is pea-size.

5. Add sour cream and milk. Mix until incorporated. Let rest for 10 minutes.

6. Roll out dough to 1 inch thickness on a lightly floured surface.

7. Using a round cutter or small juice glass, cut dough into 2 inch circles. Place on prepared baking sheet.

8. Bake at 400°F on middle rack for 5 minutes. Remove from oven and baste *(brush)* tops with melted butter. Rotate the baking sheet back to front and place on top rack in oven to ensure a nicely browned biscuit top.

9. Bake for 5 to 7 more minutes. The edges will be golden brown when done and the middle will spring back when touched lightly.

Hints

You can freeze the raw biscuits after they are cut by placing them in a single layer on a baking sheet lined with parchment paper. Place in the freezer 2 hours. Do not stack baking sheets. Store the frozen biscuits in an airtight container or large zip freezer bag.

Serve biscuits with apple butter or jam and softened butter.

Notes

Mixed Fruit

Hints

Most fruit is best when in season in your area. This may affect your choice. You can also vary this recipe depending on your personal preferences or the dietary requirements of your guests. Here are a few examples to get you started.

Notes

Ingredients

Option A	Serves 6	Serves 12	Serves 24
Strawberries *(cut)*	8 ounces	16 ounces	32 ounces
Blackberries	6 ounces	12 ounces	24 ounces
Blueberries	6 ounces	12 ounces	24 ounces

Option B	Serves 6	Serves 12	Serves 24
Fresh Pitted Cherries	8 ounces	16 ounces	32 ounces
Oranges *(sliced)*	2	4	8

Option C	Serves 6	Serves 12	Serves 24
Peaches *(peeled, sliced)*	3	6	12
Blueberries or Raspberries	8 ounces	16 ounces	32 ounces

Option D	Serves 6	Serves 12	Serves 24
Grapes *(halved)*	8 ounces	16 ounces	32 ounces
Melon *(peeled, sliced, cut into 1" cubes)*	12 ounces	24 ounces	48 ounces
Kiwi *(peeled, sliced)*	1	2	3

Method

1. Rinse fruit and drain well in a colander.

2. Prepare any fruit that needs to be peeled, cut, or sliced.

3. Keep fruit separate and add to plates as garnish. Or add all fruit to a mixing bowl and stir gently to combine.

4. Refrigerate until ready to serve.

Menu Timeline

Timing	Prep Actions
1+ days	1. Verify your supply of ingredients. Purchase any items needed to complete each recipe. Bacon can be frozen until ready to prepare. Remember to buy some vanilla or plain yogurt and a few berries for muffin garnish. Have some jam on hand to serve with the biscuits. 2. It is helpful to have the Biscuits prepared ahead. Prepare and freeze unbaked biscuits according to the recipe up to 1 month before baking. 3. Carrot Raisin Muffins can be prepared the day before serving. You may also prepare up to 1 month ahead and store in an airtight container in the freezer. Let the muffins cool completely before storing.
24+ hours	1. Remove bacon from freezer *(2 to 3 slices per guest)*. Place in refrigerator to thaw overnight. 2. Prepare muffins and biscuits according to each recipe. If these were previously prepared and frozen, remove muffins *(1 per guest)* and biscuits *(1 per guest)* from the freezer. Place in airtight containers on the counter. 3. Shred cheeses according to recipe for the number of servings. For example, 1 cup Monterey Jack and 1 cup sharp cheddar for 6 servings. 4. Begin preparations for the Farmhouse Breakfast Bowls completing steps 1 to 3. Let cool. Complete steps 5 and 6A. Cover bowls with plastic wrap and refrigerate overnight. 5. Check that your table linens are fresh and clean if you are using these. Set the table adding napkins, flatware, juice glasses, and coffee mugs. Add a selection of sweeteners in a dish, as well as salt and pepper shakers. 6. Run the dishwasher so you begin tomorrow with clean dishes and an empty dishwasher ready for the breakfast dishes.

Menu Timeline

Prep Actions		Timing

1. Turn on coffee maker. Turn on lights and music for a nice atmosphere for the cook and the guests.
2. Take farmhouse bowls out of the refrigerator and place on the counter so the dishes can come to room temperature. Allowing the dishes to come to room temperature will help prevent them from breaking when placed in a hot oven.
3. Thaw bacon, muffins, and biscuits if this was not done the day before. Place muffins on a baking sheet lined with parchment paper and cover with foil.
4. Place biscuits on separate baking sheet lined with parchment paper.

2 hours

1. Pour juices and water into pitchers. Keep in the refrigerator until serving.
2. Set the table if this was not done the day before.
3. Empty clean dishes from the dishwasher.
4. Make a pot of coffee for the cook and early risers.

1 hour **45** min

1. Preheat oven to 375°F.
2. Prepare the Tomato Basil Compote. Set aside until plating the farmhouse bowls.
3. Prepare the berry garnish for the muffin tops. Wash blueberries and strawberries. *(Plan on ½ strawberry and 3 blueberries per guest.)*

1 hour **15** min

Menu Timeline

Timing	Prep Actions

Timing

1
hour

45
min

30
min

Prep Actions

1 hour

1. Place the prepped farmhouse bowls in the oven to melt the Monterey Jack cheese.
2. Wash and prepare the mixed fruit option of your choice. Refrigerate until serving.
3. Take a moment to put away the ingredients you have finished using. Put used dishes and utensils into the dishwasher.

45 min

1. Take the farmhouse bowls out of the oven.
2. Cook bacon slices in a skillet according to the package directions. Cook slices steadily at medium heat (do not have the heat too high), turning every few minutes until bacon reaches desired crispness. HINT: Remove the bacon a bit before it reaches the desired crispness. Bacon will continue to cook for a few minutes after removed from the heat and turn out perfectly.
3. Place the bacon on a small baking sheet between layers of paper towels. Cover with foil to keep warm.

30 min

1. Place muffins in the oven for 4 to 5 minutes to warm. To avoid overheating, set a timer for 5 minutes.
2. Prepare the egg mixture for the farmhouse bowls.
3. Pour egg mixture evenly over each bowl. Top with the shredded cheddar cheese.
4. Remove muffins from oven. Allow to cool before garnishing.
5. Place jam in a pretty dish with a spoon. Set this on the table.

Menu Timeline

Prep Actions	**Timing**

Prep Actions

1. Place farmhouse bowls in the oven.
2. Place biscuits in the oven for 5 minutes.
3. Set out the plates. Add a small napkin or washable coaster to the plate for the individual bowls. This keeps the dish from slipping on the plate.

20 min

1. Remove biscuits from the oven and brush tops with melted butter. Rotate the baking sheet back to front and move to the top rack for 5 to 7 minutes until biscuits are golden brown.
2. Place juices, water, and creamer on the table.

15 min

1. Remove biscuits from oven.
2. Top muffins with yogurt and berries.
3. Add muffin, bacon, and mixed fruit to each plate.
4. Add a biscuit to each plate. Or place biscuits in a towel-lined breadbasket or bowl and place on the table.

10 min

1. Remove the farmhouse bowls from the oven.
2. Top the bowls with a generous spoonful of the tomato basil compote. Add bowl to prepared plate.

5 min

1. Serve each guest a beautiful plate.
2. Offer coffee or tea.

0 ready

MENU

Ham and Asparagus Strata
Baked Cheese Grits
Citrus Poppy Seed Loaf
Sliced Tomatoes

Ham and Asparagus Strata

Ingredients

	Serves 6	Serves 12	Serves 18
English Muffins	3	6	9
Ham	1 cup	2 cups	3 cups
Asparagus	1 cup	2 cups	3 cups
Swiss Cheese (shredded)	1½ cups	3 cups	4½ cups
Sour Cream	½ cup	1 cup	1½ cups
Onion (chopped fine)	2 Tablespoons	¼ cup	⅓ cup
Dijon Mustard	1 Tablespoon	2 Tablespoons	3 Tablespoons
Salt	⅛ teaspoon	¼ teaspoon	½ teaspoon
Pepper	⅛ teaspoon	¼ teaspoon	½ teaspoon
Eggs	4	8	12
Milk	1¾ cups	3½ cups	5¼ cups

Hints

Peeling the bottom ⅓ of an asparagus stem will give you more tender pieces.

Notes

Method

Evening Before

1. Prepare individual 10 ounce baking dishes with nonstick cooking spray. Place dishes on a baking sheet for easier handling.

2. Peel bottom ⅓ of asparagus stems. Steam asparagus for 5 to 10 minutes depending on thickness of the stems. *(Should be fork tender but not limp.)* Cool and cut into 1 inch pieces. Set aside.

3. Dice ham and set aside.

4. Tear English muffin in half, then tear the half muffin into 10 to 14 pieces. Place 5 to 7 pieces of muffin into bottom of each prepared baking dish.

5. Layer ham, asparagus, and Swiss cheese on top of muffin pieces.

6. Top with remaining English muffin pieces. Repeat process until each baking dish is filled.

7. In a small bowl, add the sour cream, onion, mustard, salt, and pepper. Stir to mix well.

8. Add the eggs and milk to the sour cream mixture and stir well.

9. Pour the egg mixture evenly over the individual dishes of strata.

10. Cover with plastic wrap and refrigerate overnight.

Next Day

11. Preheat oven to 350°F.

12. Remove strata from the refrigerator and place on the counter so the dishes can come to room temperature. Allowing the dishes to come to room temperature will help prevent them from breaking when placed in a hot oven. Remove plastic wrap.

13. Bake at 350°F for 45 to 50 minutes. Rotate the baking sheet from back to front at 20 minutes to ensure even baking.

14. When cooked, a toothpick inserted in the middle will come out clean and the top will be a rich brown color.

Baked Cheese Grits

Ingredients

	Serves 6	Serves 12	Serves 24
Water	3 cups	6 cups	12 cups
Quick Grits	¾ cup	1½ cups	3 cups
Salt	¼ teaspoon	½ teaspoon	1 teaspoon
White Pepper	dash	⅛ teaspoon	¼ teaspoon
Eggs	1	2	4
Sharp Cheddar Cheese (*shredded*)	1 cup	2 cups	4 cups
Butter	2 Tablespoons	4 Tablespoons	8 Tablespoons
Garnish			
Sharp Cheddar Cheese (*shredded*)	¼ cup	½ cup	1 cup

Method

1. Preheat oven to 350°F. Prepare individual ramekins or baking dish with nonstick cooking spray.

2. Place water and salt into a large pot and bring to a boil.

3. Whisk in the grits slowly making sure to incorporate them fully into the liquid. Reduce heat and cook until thick. Whisk often to ensure there are no lumps.

4. In a medium bowl, beat egg(s) with a fork. Add a small amount of grits to the egg(s) and stir vigorously. This step keeps the egg(s) from immediately cooking and lumping up in the hot grits.

5. Add the egg mixture to the original pot of grits and stir.

6. Add the white pepper, butter, and cheese. Stir to mix well.

7. Cook over low heat, stirring until cheese is melted and all ingredients are well combined. Remove from heat.

8. Pour or scoop into prepared ramekins or baking dish.

9. Bake at 350°F for 30 minutes until top is set and lightly puffed. Garnish with a sprinkle of cheese. Let stand for 5 minutes before serving.

Hints

This can also be prepared in a baking dish and cut into portions for serving.

An 8 x 8 baking dish can be used for 6 servings. A 9 x 13 baking dish will be needed for 12 servings.

Grits can pop and splatter while cooking. Use a pot large enough to have 2 to 3 inches of space above the cooking grits. This helps keep them in the pot and off your stovetop!

Notes

Citrus Poppy Seed Loaf

Hints

The dry and wet ingredients should be mixed together only until just combined. Overmixing the batter will result in a baked loaf with a tough texture.

Notes

Ingredients

	Makes 1 Loaf	Makes 2 Loaves	Makes 3 Loaves
All Purpose Flour	1½ cups	3 cups	4½ cups
Baking Powder	¾ teaspoon	1½ teaspoons	2¼ teaspoons
Salt	¼ teaspoon	½ teaspoon	¾ teaspoon
Eggs	2	4	6
Sugar	1 cup + 2 Tablespoons	2¼ cups	3⅓ cups
Vegetable Oil	¾ cup	1½ cups	2¼ cups
Milk	¾ cup	1½ cups	2¼ cups
Vanilla Extract	¾ teaspoon	1½ teaspoons	2¼ teaspoons
Poppy Seeds	2¼ teaspoons	4½ teaspoons	7 teaspoons
Orange Zest	1 teaspoon	2 teaspoons	3 teaspoons
Glaze			
Orange Juice	2 Tablespoons	¼ cup	⅓ cup
Powdered Sugar	⅓ cup	¾ cup	1 cup
Vanilla Extract	¼ teaspoon	½ teaspoon	¾ teaspoon

Method

1. Preheat oven to 350°F. Prepare a 5 x 9 loaf pan with nonstick baking spray.

2. Using a whisk, mix the flour, baking powder, and salt in a large mixing bowl until well combined. Set aside.

3. Add eggs and sugar to a medium mixing bowl. Using a hand mixer, beat eggs and sugar together until fluffy. Mixture will be double the original volume.

4. Drizzle in the oil while continuing to beat.

5. Add the milk, vanilla, poppy seeds, and orange zest to the egg mixture. Mix until thoroughly combined.

6. Add the dry ingredients to the egg mixture. Mix by hand only until just combined.

7. Pour batter into loaf pan.

8. Bake at 350°F for 1 hour. Rotate the pan in the oven back to front after 25 minutes for even baking. The loaf will spring back from a gentle touch on the top when done. A toothpick inserted in the center will come out clean.

9. Let loaf cool for 10 minutes before removing from the pan.

10. The loaf can be prepared the day before serving. You may also prepare up to 1 month ahead and store in an airtight container in the freezer. Let the loaf cool completely before storing.

11. Before serving, combine the orange juice, powdered sugar, and vanilla extract.

12. Drizzle loaf with the orange juice glaze.

Notes

Menu Timeline

Timing	Prep Actions

Timing

1+
days

Prep Actions

1. Verify your supply of ingredients. Purchase any items needed to complete each recipe. Have some fresh ripe tomatoes on hand for slicing.

2. Citrus Poppy Seed Loaf can be prepared the day before serving. You may also prepare up to 1 month ahead and store in an airtight container in the freezer. Let the loaf cool completely before storing.

24+
hours

1. All the components of this menu are prepared the day before. This makes the morning of serving easier for you!

2. Prepare the loaf according to the recipe and cool. If previously prepared and frozen, remove the loaf *(1 per 6 guests)* from the freezer. Place the loaf in an airtight container on the counter.

3. Prepare the Ham and Asparagus Strata according the recipe through step 10. Cover dishes with plastic wrap and refrigerate overnight.

4. Prepare Baked Cheese Grits according to the recipe through step 10. Place in prepared individual ramekins or baking dish. Individual ramekins should be placed on a baking sheet for easier handling. Grits will be baked in the morning. Cover with plastic wrap and refrigerate overnight.

5. Check that your table linens are fresh and clean if you are using these. Set the table adding napkins, flatware, juice glasses, and coffee mugs. Add a selection of sweeteners in a dish, as well as salt and pepper shakers.

1 **30**
hour min

1. Preheat oven to 350°F.

2. Turn on coffee maker. Turn on lights and music for a nice atmosphere for the cook and the guests.

3. Remove the prepared dishes of strata and grits from the refrigerator and place on the counter. Allowing the dishes to come to room temperature will help prevent them from breaking when placed in a hot oven.

Menu Timeline

Prep Actions	**Timing**

1. Remove the loaf from the airtight container and place on a baking sheet lined with parchment paper. Cover with foil.

1 hour 15 min

2. Pour juices and water into pitchers. Keep in the refrigerator until serving.

3. Set the table if this was not done the day before.

4. Make a pot of coffee for the cook and early risers.

1. Remove plastic wrap and place the strata in the oven.

1 hour

2. Empty clean dishes from the dishwasher.

1. Remove plastic wrap and place the grits in the oven.

45 min

2. Set out the plates. Add a small coaster or cocktail napkin to the plate if using individual dishes. This keeps the dish from sliding around on the plate.

3. Rotate strata baking sheet in the oven from back to front for even baking.

1. Slice tomatoes and place on paper towels. Sprinkle with a little salt. This will keep the juices from running on the plate.

30 min

2. Take a moment to put away the ingredients you have finished using. Put used dishes and utensils into the dishwasher.

Menu Timeline

Timing	Prep Actions

Timing

Prep Actions

20
min

1. Rotate the strata.
2. Place the loaf in the oven for 3 to 7 minutes to warm. To avoid overheating, set a timer for 7 minutes.
3. Prepare Orange Glaze.
4. Remove the loaf from the oven and allow to cool slightly. Remove from pan. Drizzle warm loaf with the orange glaze.

10
min

1. Place juices, water, and creamer on the table.
2. Remove strata from the oven. It will be bubbly around the edges and light golden brown on top when done.
3. Remove grits from the oven.
4. Prepare each plate with a serving of strata, a serving of grits, sliced tomatoes, and 2 slices of the loaf. *(Glaze makes loaf a bit of a mess to serve from a breadbasket.)*

0
ready

1. Serve each guest a beautiful plate.
2. Offer coffee or tea.

MENU

Sausage Apple Puff Pancake

Gingerbread Scones
with Lemon Butter

Cherry Almond Granola
with Orange Yogurt

Sausage Apple Puff Pancake

Ingredients

	Serves 6	Serves 12	Serves 24
Bulk Sausage (crumbled, cooked, drained)	1 pound	2 pounds	4 pounds
Apples (peeled, sliced)	6	12	24
Butter	2 ounces (½ stick)	4 ounces (1 stick)	8 ounces (2 sticks)
Brown Sugar (packed)	¼ cup	½ cup	1 cup
All Purpose Flour	1 cup	2 cups	4 cups
Sugar	2 Tablespoons	¼ cup	½ cup
Salt	½ teaspoon	1 teaspoon	2 teaspoons
Eggs	6	12	24
Milk	1½ cups	3 cups	6 cups
Sharp Cheddar Cheese (shredded)	1 cup	2 cups	4 cups

Hints

Stirring apples too frequently or too long will result in applesauce.

Use Granny Smith or other firm cooking apple variety.

Place individual skillets on a baking sheet for easier handling.

One 10 inch skillet or six 5 inch skillets are needed per 6 servings. These should be cast iron.

Notes

Method

1. Preheat oven to 425°F. Grease 6 small cast iron skillets or 1 large cast iron skillet with a bit of oil. Place small skillets on baking sheets for easier handling.

2. In a large skillet, crumble sausage and cook throughly. Drain fat.

3. Wash apples, peel and quarter. Remove the core from each quarter, then slice each quarter into 4 slices.

4. In a large skillet, heat butter on medium until bubbly. Add sliced apples and brown sugar. Cook on low until apples are tender but not mushy. Set aside.

5. Using a fork or whisk, combine the flour, sugar, and salt in a medium bowl. Add eggs and milk. Stir to combine.

6. Evenly divide the apples between the mini skillets, or spread over the bottom of the 10 inch skillet.

7. Pour the batter over the apples. Sprinkle each dish with the sausage and then with the shredded sharp cheddar cheese.

8. Bake at 425°F for 20 minutes for mini skillets, 30 minutes for 10 inch skillet. The top will puff up and become a rich brown color when done.

Gingerbread Scones

Ingredients

	Makes 12	Makes 24	Makes 36
All Purpose Flour	2¼ cups	4½ cups	6¾ cups
Baking Powder	1 teaspoon	2 teaspoons	1 Tablespoon
Baking Soda	¼ teaspoon	½ teaspoon	¾ teaspoon
Cinnamon	1 teaspoon	2 teaspoons	1 Tablespoon
Ginger	½ teaspoon	1 teaspoon	1½ teaspoons
Allspice	¼ teaspoon	½ teaspoon	¾ teaspoon
Nutmeg	¼ teaspoon	½ teaspoon	¾ teaspoon
Butter (cold)	½ cup	1 cup	1½ cups
Heavy Cream	¾ cup	1½ cups	2¼ cups
Molasses	½ cup	1 cup	1½ cups
Raisins (soaked)	½ cup	1 cup	1½ cups

Hints

The dry and wet ingredients should be mixed together only until just combined. Overmixing the batter will result in baked scones with a tough texture.

The scones can be prepared the day before serving. You may also prepare up to 1 month ahead and store in an airtight container in the freezer. Let the scones cool completely before storing.

Notes

Method

1. Preheat oven to 400°F. Line a baking sheet with parchment paper.

2. Place raisins in a stainless steel or glass bowl. Pour boiling water over the raisins, enough to cover. Set aside to soak.

3. Using a whisk, mix the flour, baking powder, baking soda, cinnamon, ginger, allspice, and nutmeg in a large mixing bowl until well combined.

4. Slice the butter into tablespoon-size pieces and add to the flour mixture. Using a pastry cutter, cut the butter pieces into the dry ingredients until the butter is pea-size.

5. Drain the raisins. Add the heavy cream, molasses, and the raisins to the flour mixture. Mix until just combined.

6. Turn out the dough onto a lightly floured surface and divide in half.

7. Roll each half into an 8 inch circle about ½ inch thick.

8. Cut the dough circles into 6 equal pie-shaped wedges and place on the baking sheet.

9. Bake at 400°F for 10 to 12 minutes. Rotate the baking sheet back to front at 5 minutes for even baking. Scones will appear slightly moist and very lightly brown when done.

10. Let the scones cool for 10 minutes before serving. Serve with Lemon Butter.

11. The scones can be prepared the day before serving. You many also prepare up to 1 month ahead and store in an airtight container in the freezer. Let the scones cool completely before storing.

Lemon Butter

Notes

Ingredients

	Makes ½ Cup	Makes 1 Cup	Makes 1½ Cups
Butter (*room temperature*)	4 ounces (*1 stick*)	8 ounces (*2 sticks*)	12 ounces (*3 sticks*)
Lemon Zest	1 Tablespoon	2 Tablespoons	3 Tablespoons
Lemon Juice	2 Tablespoons	4 Tablespoons	6 Tablespoons
Powdered Sugar	1 Tablespoon	2 Tablespoons	3 Tablespoons

Method

1. Place all ingredients in a mixing bowl. Using a hand mixer, mix until well combined.

2. Scrape down the sides of the bowl several times with a spatula while mixing to incorporate all the butter.

3. Lemon butter can be prepared ahead and stored in an airtight container in the refrigerator for 1 month. Soften before using.

Orange Yogurt

Ingredients

Notes

	Serves 6	Serves 12	Serves 24
Greek Vanilla Yogurt	1½ cups	3 cups	6 cups
Orange Juice	¼ cup	½ cup	1 cup
Orange Zest	1 Tablespoon	2 Tablespoons	4 Tablespoons

Method

1. Mix all ingredients together in a large bowl.

2. Divide evenly between individual ramekins or small serving bowls.

Cherry Almond Granola

Hints

Granola can be frozen in an airtight container for 1 month. Thaw before serving.

Notes

Ingredients

	Makes 3 Cups	Makes 6 Cups	Makes 9 Cups
Old-Fashioned Oats	2 cups	4 cups	6 cups
Unsweetened Shredded Coconut	½ cup	1 cup	1½ cups
Sliced Almonds	½ cup	1 cup	1½ cups
Brown Sugar *(packed)*	2 Tablespoons	4 Tablespoons	6 Tablespoons
Cinnamon	½ teaspoon	1 teaspoon	1½ teaspoons
Salt	¼ teaspoon	½ teaspoon	¾ teaspoon
Coconut Oil	¼ cup	½ cup	¾ cup
Maple Syrup	½ cup	1 cup	1½ cups
Vanilla Extract	½ teaspoon	1 teaspoon	1½ teaspoons
Dried Cherries	½ cup	1 cup	1½ cups

Method

1. Preheat oven to 300°F. Line a baking sheet with parchment paper.

2. In a large mixing bowl, mix the oats, coconut, almonds, brown sugar, cinnamon, and salt until well combined.

3. In a small saucepan, heat the coconut oil until melted. Remove from heat. Add the maple syrup and vanilla extract to the coconut oil, and mix well.

4. Pour the coconut oil mixture over the oats and combine well. Mix until all the oats are coated uniformly.

5. Spread the oat mixture evenly over prepared baking sheet.

6. Bake at 300°F for 30 minutes. Stir every 10 minutes. The mixture will be deep golden brown when done. Granola will not be crunchy until it has cooled for at least 20 minutes.

7. Once cooled completely, stir in the dried cherries.

8. Store in an airtight container. Enjoy!

Menu Timeline

Prep Actions	Timing

Prep Actions

1. Verify your supply of ingredients. Purchase any items needed to complete the recipe. Bulk sausage can be frozen until ready to prepare.
2. Gingerbread Scones can prepared the day before serving. You may also prepare up to 1 month ahead and store in an airtight container in the freezer. Let the scones cool completely before storing.
3. Lemon Butter can be prepared ahead and stored in the refrigerator for several weeks.

1+ days

1. Remove sausage *(1 pound per 6 servings)* from the freezer. Place in the refrigerator to thaw overnight.
2. Prepare scones according to the recipe. If these were previously prepared and frozen, remove scones *(1 to 2 per guest)* from the freezer. Place scones in an airtight container on the counter.
3. Prepare lemon butter if this was not done previously.
4. Check that your table linens are fresh and clean if you are using these. Set the table adding napkins, flatware, juice glasses, and coffee mugs. Add a selection of sweeteners in a dish, as well as salt and pepper shakers.
5. Run the dishwasher so you begin tomorrow with clean dishes and an empty dishwasher ready for all of the breakfast dishes.

24+ hours

1. Turn on coffee maker. Turn on lights and music for a nice atmosphere for the cook and the guests.
2. Thaw sausage if this was not done the day before.
3. Remove lemon butter from the refrigerator to soften.
4. Place scones on a baking sheet lined with parchment paper and cover with foil.

2 hours

Menu Timeline

Timing	Prep Actions

Timing

Prep Actions

1 hour **45** min

1. Pour juices and water into pitchers. Keep in the refrigerator until serving.
2. Set the table if this was not done the day before.
3. Empty clean dishes from the dishwasher.
4. Make a pot of coffee for the cook and early risers.

1 hour **30** min

1. In a large skillet, crumble sausage and cook throughly. Drain fat.
2. Peel and slice apples.

1 hour

1. Preheat oven to 425°F.
2. Prepare Orange Yogurt according to the recipe. Place in small bowls or ramekins. Place these on a tray or baking sheet. Cover with plastic wrap and refrigerate.

45 min

1. Prepare the egg mixture for the Sausage Apple Puff Pancakes according to the recipe.
2. Assemble the pancake ingredients in prepared skillets as described in the recipe. Individual skillets should be placed on baking sheets for easier handling.
3. If serving in a 10 inch skillet, place in the oven for 35 minutes.

Menu Timeline

Prep Actions	Timing
1. Set out the plates. Add a small napkin or washable coaster to each plate if using the 5 inch skillets. This will help protect the plate from the very hot skillet. 2. If using 5 inch skillets, place in the oven for 25 minutes.	**30** min
1. Rotate the pancake skillets in the oven back to front for even baking. 2. Place juices, water, creamer, and lemon butter on the table. 3. Top the orange yogurt bowls with the Cherry Almond Granola. Place these on the table above the fork at each place setting.	**15** min
1. Remove the pancake skillets from the oven. Pancakes should be puffed up and a rich brown color. 2. Place scones in the oven for 3 to 4 minutes to warm. To avoid overheating, set a timer for 4 minutes. 3. Place individual skillets on a coaster or napkin on each plate. Or serve portions from the big skillet directly onto each plate. 4. Remove scones from oven. 5. Add a scone to each plate. Or place these in a towel-lined breadbasket or bowl and place on the table.	**5** min
1. Serve each guest a beautiful plate. Let guests know the skillets are just from the oven and very hot. 2. Offer coffee or tea.	**0** ready

MENU

Bacon Blue Cheese Quiche

White Chocolate
Cranberry Scones

Arugula Salad with
Walnut Vinaigrette

Roasted Red Potatoes

Bacon Blue Cheese Quiche

Ingredients

	Serves 6	Serves 12	Serves 18
Puff Pastry (thawed)	1 sheet	2 sheets	3 sheets
Bacon (chopped, cooked)	8 pieces	1 pound	1½ pounds
Onion (medium diced)	½ cup	1 cup	1½ cups
Blue Cheese (crumbled)	⅓ cup	⅔ cup	1 cup
Eggs	10	20	30
Heavy Cream	1 cup	2 cups	3 cups
Parmesan Cheese (shredded)	½ cup	1 cup	1½ cups
Salt	½ teaspoon	1 teaspoon	1½ teaspoons
Nutmeg	¼ teaspoon	½ teaspoon	¾ teaspoon
Black Pepper	½ teaspoon	1 teaspoon	1½ teaspoons
Bosc or Anjou Pears - Medium (sliced thin)	2	4	6
Butter	2 Tablespoons	4 Tablespoons	6 Tablespoons
Brown Sugar (packed)	1 Tablespoon	2 Tablespoons	3 Tablespoons

Hints

This is a great quiche to serve for a brunch or light dinner.

The blue cheese in this recipe provides a rich but surprisingly subtle flavor profile. Don't let it scare you if you're not normally a fan of blue cheese!

Notes

Method

1. Preheat oven to 350°F.

2. Cut bacon into small pieces with kitchen scissors. Dice the onion.

3. In a large skillet, cook bacon for about 5 minutes on medium heat.

4. Add onion and continue cooking until the onion is golden and the bacon is crispy and brown.

5. Drain off the excess fat from the skillet and set mixture aside.

6. In a medium mixing bowl, mix the blue cheese, eggs, heavy cream, Parmesan cheese, salt, nutmeg, and black pepper until well combined.

7. In a separate skillet, heat butter on low until melted. Sauté sliced pears for 6 to 7 minutes on low heat. Stir lightly and infrequently. Add brown sugar to pears and continue to cook for 2 more minutes.

8. Prepare a 10 inch spring form pan or individual 10 ounce baking dishes with nonstick baking spray.

9. Press the thawed puff pastry into the bottom of the prepared pan or individual baking dishes. Place individual dishes on a baking sheet for easier handling.

10. Sprinkle the crispy bacon and onion mixture evenly over the puff pastry.

11. Spread the sliced pears evenly over the bacon.

12. Pour the egg mixture over the pears.

13. Bake at 350°F for 20 to 30 minutes for individual dishes. Bake 30 to 40 minutes for a 10 inch spring form pan. Quiche will be firm in the center when done.

14. Let rest 5 to 10 minutes before cutting or serving.

White Chocolate Cranberry Scones

Ingredients

	Makes 8	Makes 16	Makes 24
All Purpose Flour	2 cups	4 cups	6 cups
Sugar	⅓ cup	⅔ cup	1 cup
Baking Powder	1 teaspoon	2 teaspoons	1 Tablespoon
Baking Soda	¼ teaspoon	½ teaspoon	¾ teaspoon
Salt	½ teaspoon	1 teaspoon	1½ teaspoons
Butter	4 ounces (1 stick)	8 ounces (2 sticks)	12 ounces (3 sticks)
Dried Cranberries	½ cup	1 cup	1½ cups
White Chocolate Chips	½ cup	1 cup	1½ cups
Sour Cream	½ cup	1 cup	1½ cups
Eggs	1	2	3

Hints

The dry and wet ingredients should be mixed together only until just combined. Overmixing the batter will result in baked scones with a tough texture.

Notes

Method

1. Preheat oven to 400°F. Line a baking sheet with parchment paper.

2. Using a whisk, mix the flour, sugar, baking powder, baking soda, and salt in a large mixing bowl until well combined.

3. Slice the butter into tablespoon-size pieces and add to the flour mixture. Using a pastry cutter, cut the butter pieces into the dry ingredients until the butter is pea-size.

4. In a small bowl, combine the dried cranberries and white chocolate chips. Add to the flour mixture, and mix well.

5. In a separate bowl, whisk egg(s) and sour cream vigorously to incorporate air and blend together.

6. Add sour cream mixture to flour mixture. Mix until just combined.

7. Turn out dough onto a lightly floured surface. Shape into a circle and roll out to 1 inch thick.

8. Cut the dough circle into 8 pie-shaped wedges. Place wedges on the baking sheet.

9. Bake at 400°F for 15 to 17 minutes. Rotate the baking sheet back to front at 7 minutes for even baking. Scones will appear slightly moist and very light brown when done.

10. Let the scones cool for 10 minutes before serving.

11. The scones can be prepared the day before serving. You may also prepare up to 1 month ahead and store in an airtight container in the freezer. Let the scones cool completely before storing.

Arugula Salad with Walnut Vinaigrette

Ingredients

	Serves 6	Serves 12	Serves 24
Arugula	3 cups	6 cups	12 cups
Vinaigrette			
Toasted Walnuts (*chopped*)	¼ cup	½ cup	1 cup
Shallots (*chopped*)	1 Tablespoon	2 Tablespoons	¼ cup
White Balsamic Vinegar	2 Tablespoons	¼ cup	½ cup
Water	1 Tablespoon	2 Tablespoons	¼ cup
Salt	½ teaspoon	1 teaspoon	2 teaspoons
Black Pepper	⅛ teaspoon	¼ teaspoon	½ teaspoon
Brown Sugar	¾ teaspoon	1½ teaspoons	1 Tablespoon
Olive Oil	2 Tablespoons	¼ cup	½ cup
Walnut Oil	2 Tablespoons	¼ cup	½ cup

Hints

There may be leftover vinaigrette. Refrigerate for 2 months.

Notes

Method

1. Preheat oven to 350°F. Line a baking sheet with parchment paper.

2. Place walnuts on the baking sheet. Bake at 350°F for 5 to 7 minutes. Set a timer as these can quickly burn. Set aside to cool.

3. Using a whisk, mix walnuts, shallots, vinegar, water, salt, pepper, and brown sugar in a medium mixing bowl until well combined.

4. Whisk the olive and walnut oils into the mixture until incorporated.

5. Set vinaigrette aside.

6. Wash arugula and spin or pat dry. Break up any large pieces and place in large mixing bowl.

7. Drizzle vinaigrette over arugula, tossing the greens with tongs until lightly coated.

8. Serve cold.

Roasted Red Potatoes

Ingredients

	Serves 6	Serves 12	Serves 18
Red Bliss Potatoes	30 small	60 small	90 small
Olive oil	2 Tablespoons	¼ cup	⅓ cup
Salt	¾ teaspoon	1½ teaspoons	2¼ teaspoons
Pepper	½ teaspoon	1 teaspoon	1½ teaspoons

Method

1. Preheat oven to 350°F. Line a baking sheet with parchment paper.
2. Wash potatoes and pat dry.
3. Cut potatoes in half. This will result in 10 halves per guest.
4. In a large bowl, toss the diced potatoes with the olive oil, salt, and pepper.
5. Evenly scatter the potatoes over prepared baking sheet.
6. Bake at 350°F for 45 to 50 minutes. Stir potatoes and rotate baking sheet every 15 minutes.

Menu Timeline

Prep Actions	Timing

Prep Actions

1. Verify your supply of ingredients. Purchase any items needed to complete each recipe. Bacon may be frozen until ready to prepare.

2. White Chocolate Cranberry Scones can be prepared the day before serving. You may also prepare up to 1 month ahead and store in an airtight container in the freezer. Let the scones cool completely before storing.

1+ days

1. Prepare scones according to the recipe and cool. If these were previously prepared and frozen, remove scones *(1 per guest)* from the freezer. Place scones in an airtight container on the counter.

2. Chop and cook the bacon and onion needed for the Bacon Blue Cheese Quiche. Place in the refrigerator in an airtight container.

3. Make the Walnut Vinaigrette and refrigerate.

4. Check that your table linens are fresh and clean if you are using these. Set the table adding napkins, flatware, juice glasses, and coffee mugs. Add a selection of sweeteners in a dish, as well salt and pepper shakers.

5. Run the dishwasher so you begin tomorrow with clean dishes and an empty dishwasher ready for all of the breakfast dishes.

24+ hours

1. Turn on coffee maker. Turn on lights and music for a nice atmosphere for the cook and the guests.

2. Place scones on a baking sheet lined with parchment paper and cover with foil.

3. Chop and cook the bacon and onion if this was not done the day before.

2 hours

Menu Timeline

Timing	Prep Actions

Timing

Prep Actions

1 hour **45** min

1. Pour juices and water into pitchers. Keep in the refrigerator until serving.
2. Set the table if this was not done the day before.
3. Empty clean dishes from the dishwasher.
4. Wash arugula and set aside to dry.
5. Make a pot of coffee for the cook and early risers.

1 hour **30** min

1. Prepare the baking pan or individual dishes and line with the puff pastry.
2. Spoon bacon and onion mixture evenly over the pastry.
3. Prepare the egg mixture for the quiche according to the recipe.

1 hour **15** min

1. Preheat oven to 350°F.
2. Slice the pears. Sauté according to the recipe. Evenly spread the pears over bacon and onions.
3. Pour the egg mixture over top of the pears.

1 hour

1. Place the quiche in the oven.
2. Prepare the Roasted Red Potatoes according to the recipe.

45 min

1. Place potatoes in the oven.
2. Set out the plates. Add a small napkin or washable coaster to the plate for the individual dishes. This keeps the dish from slipping on the plate and protects from the very hot dishes.
3. Remove the Walnut Vinaigrette from the refrigerator.

Menu Timeline

Prep Actions	Timing

Prep Actions   **Timing**

1. Stir the potatoes.
2. Check the quiche. It will be firm in the center when done. It will likely need a few more minutes.
3. Take a moment to put away the ingredients you have finished using. Put used dishes and utensils into the dishwasher.
4. Toss arugula with the walnut vinaigrette.

30 min

1. Remove quiche from the oven when done. Let rest 5 to 10 minutes before slicing if using a large pan.
2. Stir the potatoes.
3. Place scones in the oven for 5 to 7 minutes to warm. To avoid overheating, set a timer for 7 minutes.
4. Place individual quiche dishes on a coaster or napkin on each plate.
5. Remove scones from oven.

15 min

1. Place juices, water, and creamer on the table.
2. Remove potatoes from oven.
3. Prepare each plate with a slice of the quiche *(if serving from large pan)* and 10 potato halves. Add a serving of the salad.
4. Add a scone to each plate. Or place these in a towel-lined breadbasket or bowl and place on the table.

5 min

1. Serve each guest a beautiful plate.
2. Offer coffee or tea.

0 ready

A Note About the Authors

Darlene grew up learning to cook with her mother and grandmother. In middle school, Darlene clipped recipes from newspapers, building files and imagining how the final outcome of the recipes would taste. This early practice led to the ability to be creative in the kitchen if not always exact. If you have ever worked in the kitchen with her, you know measurements are loosely followed and there may be a secret ingredient or two. She completed several culinary courses before turning her attention to her love of science which gave more precision to her cooking practice and organization.

She continued a love of cooking and baking, using her kitchen to find ways to serve others resulting in many culinary adventures. None of these were quite as audacious as the adventure of designing, building, and operating a country inn and conference center with her husband Norman in Middle Tennessee. Tens of thousands of meals were served around their table. The memories of Butterfly Meadows Inn & Farm will always hold a special place in her heart, and she is delighted to be able to share with you the collection of recipes that were enjoyed by so many there and the methods developed for success in the kitchen.

Darlene longs for the day when she sits at her Lord's table and desires greatly to meet or reacquaint with you there.

Kelly has been a food lover from the beginning. She grew up enjoying home-cooked meals and watching her mom experiment in the kitchen. By seventh grade she knew that working with food would be in her future. She began making wedding cakes for friends and family while she was in high school. Some of her creations were complete disasters (think frosting flowers falling off the cake the entire way to the wedding) and yet she still dreamed of the culinary world. She started working in restaurants at the age of 14. Kelly graduated from the Culinary Institute of America. She worked as a pastry chef for several years, then fulfilled a lifelong dream of decorating wedding cakes professionally. She opened her own bakery in upstate New York before her move to Tennessee.

When Kelly stepped into the culinary team at Butterfly Meadows Inn, she knew she was among her people. From the first meeting, there was an instant connection with Darlene. A collaboration began and a lifelong friendship was established. Kelly considers being in the kitchen with the people she cares about a special gift from the Lord!

Along with cooking food, Kelly is passionate about growing food and learning the skills needed to be food self-sufficient. She lives on a farm with her husband Tim and son Jacob, enjoying the goodness that our awesome God grows around them.

Special Thanks

We cannot begin to say enough thanks to our fellow collaborators on this project. M.E. Hall and Rosemary Hilliard, your exceptional talent, skill, and gracefully applied polish have been invaluable. You made this book shine. Your laughter, love, friendship, and the way you walk through life with your people are a cherished treasure!

Recommendation

Gracious Goodness Around the Table: Breakfast is the perfect cookery book for anyone, whether a first time cook or a professional chef. This book is a labor of love built on the love of good food and sharing that love with others. The menus and recipes are well thought out and easy to follow. The timelines will give you confidence to prepare and present a delicious breakfast to your guests.

I was very pleased to be asked to write a note to accompany this new cookery book as I have had the privilege of gathering around the table with Darlene and Kelly and enjoying wonderful meals they have prepared. Now you can have the benefit of their expertise to share with those you gather around your table.

Dr. David Woodfine
Master, Oxford City Guild of Chefs
High Steward (Retired), Harris Manchester College, University of Oxford

Equipment List

Essentials

Mixing Spoons
(silicone or wooden)

8″ Chef's Knife

Paring Knife

Kitchen Scissors

½ Cup (#8) Squeeze
Release Scoop *(ice cream type)*

2 Tablespoon (#40)
Squeeze Release Scoop

Measuring Cup Set

Measuring Spoon Set

Liquid Measuring Cups
(1 cup, 2 cup)

Whisk

Spatula

Pastry Brush

Tongs

Small Fine Mesh Strainer

Vegetable Peeler

2″ Biscuit Cutter or Glass

Grater

Small and Large Colanders

Mixing Bowl Set
(3 or 4 bowls)

Cutting Board

Handheld Electric Mixer

Freezer Bags

Plastic Wrap

Aluminum Foil

Parchment Paper

10 Ounce Oven Safe Bakeware -
Pyrex or similar *(1 per guest)*

8 x 8 Baking Dish

9 x 13 Baking Dish

Baking Sheets *(2)*

12 Cup Regular Size Muffin Pan

6 Cup Regular Size Muffin Pan

24 Cup Mini Muffin Pan

10″ Round Glass or
Ceramic Pie Plate

5 x 9 Loaf Baking Pan
(metal, glass, or ceramic)

10″ Springform Pan

Small Skillet *(8″ or 10″)*

Large Skillet *(12″ or 14″)*

Saucepans with Lids
(1 quart, 2 quart)

4 Quart Pot with Lid

Extras

Stand Mixer with Paddle and Whisk
Attachments

16 Cup Sterilite Rectangle Airtight
Food Storage Containers
*(A container will hold 1 dozen
regular size muffins or 2 dozen mini
muffins. Purchase as many as needed
to store or freeze all items.)*

4 Ounce Ceramic Ramekins
(1 per guest)

8 Ounce Ceramic Ramekins
(1 per guest)

5 x 7 Glass or Ceramic Baking
Dishes *(1 per guest)*

5″ Tart Pans *(1 per guest)*

Liquid Measuring Cups
(4 cup, 8 cup)

Baking Sheets *(2 to 4 extra)*

Muffin Pans *(2 extra)*

Mini Muffin Pan *(1 extra)*

10″ Tart Pan

Mini Loaf Baking Pans *(1 to 2)*

5″ Cast Iron Skillets *(1 per guest)*

8 Quart Pot with Lid
(for larger quantities)

Index

Index

Index